RESOLVING CONFLICT IN THE BLENDED FAMILY

Also by the authors:
The Blended Family

RESOLVING CONFLICT IN THE BLENDED FAMILY

TOM & ADRIENNE FRYDENGER

√ chosen books

FLEMING H. REVELL COMPANY
TARRYTOWN, NEW YORK

Scripture texts are from the Holy Bible, New International Version, Copyright © 1973, 1978, 1984 International Bible Society. Used by permission of Zondervan Bible Publishers.

The chart on page 128 is taken from *Old Loyalties, New Ties* by Visher and Visher, published by Brunner/ Mazel, Inc., 1988, and is used with permission.

Library of Congress Cataloging-in-Publication Data

Frydenger, Tom.
   Resolving conflict in the blended family / Tom and Adrienne
   Frydenger.
      p. cm.
   ISBN 0-8007-9182-7
   1. Family—Religious life. 2. Remarriage—Religious aspects—
   Christianity. I. Frydenger, Adrienne. II. Title.
   BV4526.2.F792   1991
   248.4—dc20   91-18028   CIP

A Chosen book
Copyright © 1991 by Tom and Adrienne Frydenger
Chosen Books Publishing Company, Ltd.
Published by
Fleming H. Revell Company
Tarrytown, New York
Printed in the United States of America

To all the stepfamilies
who have attended our seminars
and given us new perspectives on how
to make blended families work.

Contents

Introduction: "You've Got to Be Kidding!"

"Have a happy family? We don't even resemble a family."

"At this point, I really don't want to do anything that requires any level of sacrifice for me or my children. Why should we try, just to be put down or disappointed again?"

What makes these blended family members so unwilling to cooperate? Why won't they budge? Why do they refuse even to try? We discovered that the answer lay in their deep-seated resentments and belief that nothing will ever change.

But hurt, unresolved conflict and disappointment, my dear blended family friend, do not have to continue to be part of your everyday life. There is hope, healing and healthy family living in God's plan for your blended family.

When Chosen Books asked us to write *The Blended Family*, it was due to Adrienne's writing ability, my being a Christian family and marriage counselor and our living in a blended family. The last of these *obviously* made us experts! Right? Little did we know how little we knew.

Within the next year we read every book and article we could find on blended families. And voilà! *The Blended Family* was created. Upon its publication, we were acknowledged as "the experts," especially in the Christian community. We were guests on "Focus on the Family," "The 700 Club," "Straight Talk" and a variety of other radio and television programs; and we also began doing blended family seminars around the country. It was while doing these seminars, and through the increased number of blended families I was counseling, that we began to see the real need for this book.

The Blended Family lays out some excellent plans on how to make a blended family work (if we do say so ourselves!). If you and/or other family members are struggling with resentments, however, stuck in a rut, can't get other family members to cooperate, or are just burned out on blended family life, this book is for you. In it you will find out how to let go of your resentments, learn practical guidelines for resolving conflict and discover how to foster teamwork within your blended family.

After a series of setbacks (which was more the norm than the exception to the rule), we received an early morning phone call from our pastor. This is what he said:

"The Lord woke me in the middle of the night and let me know very specifically that I was to encourage you in the writing of your book. He also impressed upon me that this book will be ministering to blended families after you and Adrienne are long gone."

That is our hope—that this book will indeed continue to be an avenue of healing and wholeness for many blended families—including yours.

RESOLVING CONFLICT IN THE BLENDED FAMILY

— 1 —
Straight Talk

"Hi, I'm Michelle, guest coordinator for the Christian Broadcasting Network's television program 'Straight Talk,' with Scott Ross. Our producers would like to invite you and your husband, Tom, to be guests on a one-day show dealing with the perils of stepparenting. Your book, *The Blended Family,* has helped so many people, and we thought you'd be naturals."

"Sounds wonderful," replied my wife, Adrienne, knowing how much I enjoy an occasional break from my counseling practice. "Let me check with Tom and we'll get back to you." As we discussed the invitation later, we were excited about the prospect of sharing with others what we have learned and lived through as a blended family.

A few days later Michelle called again. Would we consider being on the program for two days, with the second day focusing on stepchildren and their reactions to living in a blended family?

"We'd love to," Adrienne responded quickly.

"Great!" said Michelle. "We have two stepbrothers, Jason

and Mark, who are close in age and living in a very positive stepfamily situation, and a young girl, Lisa, who had a bad experience with her stepmother. Now we need someone in the middle—someone who has experienced both the positive and negative sides of blended family living. Do you think your older daughter fits this category, and would she consider being a guest on the program?"

This time Adrienne was not so quick to respond.

Nichole, one of Adrienne's two daughters from her previous marriage, had been back home with us (Adrienne and I also have a son together) for a year after having lived with her father for two years. The difficulties that had led to her moving out of our home after high school and into her father's house seemed to have been resolved, although lately the boat had been rocking.

When Nichole, then nineteen, asked to move back home, we discussed with her the household rules Adrienne and I had agreed upon. "No problem," she said.

In my opinion, the rules were simple and fair. Nichole was to: help with household chores; keep her room clean; be in by curfew—10:30 weeknights (we all had to get up early) and 1:00 weekends; pay $20 a week rent; treat family members with respect; and (just in case) refrain from smoking and drinking.

But lately Nichole had had things other than our household rules on her mind. She had become engaged to her high school sweetheart at Christmas and was planning a wedding for the last weekend in July. In addition, she and her fiancé, David, were busy renovating a home they had bought, and chores at our house were not high on her priority list. Her room was a wreck, stacked with miscellaneous items that would go into her home when it was ready, and piled high with dirty clothes and half-empty iced tea glasses. She made it home by curfew less and less often, and she paid her rent sporadically.

When the call for "Straight Talk" came in May, wedding plans were in full swing, the kids were working on their house full steam ahead, and it seemed more and more that Adrienne's and my discussions about Nichole's choices wound up in arguments.

As Adrienne and I worked through those conflicts, Nichole fluctuated between excitement about appearing on national TV and panic. As the scheduled date for the program approached, she became more anxious and increasingly distant. The week before the program she occupied herself with wedding plans and put off packing until just two hours before our flight time, which made her mother a nervous wreck.

As we flew to Virginia Beach, Adrienne and Nichole chatted about the program. Nichole was on a negative roll.

"I can't believe I said I would do this. Mom, isn't there any way I can get out of this?"

"No, absolutely not," Adrienne said firmly, then added reassuringly, "but everything will work out just fine."

Nichole was not that easily encouraged. "I wish you and Dad had never written that book about blended families!"

Adrienne was not too surprised at Nichole's comment, but it suddenly gave her a funny feeling.

"Nichole, what are you planning to talk about on the program?"

Nichole shook her head, replying only, "You and Dad are going to hate me after this."

At that point I decided Nichole was going to say something on "Straight Talk" that was not going to make me happy, and I began preparing myself for the worst. Because Nichole had distanced herself from us, I concluded that she must be mulling over old, possibly unresolved, resentments.

I began asking myself all sorts of questions. What had she resented or what did she still resent? The household rules? Maybe as she reflected in preparation for this program, she began thinking we were too strict . . . too hard. Or that *I* was too strict. . . .

The first day of the programming went well. Out in the audience Nichole appeared more relaxed, less anxious. Although Adrienne and I were still a little uneasy about the mysterious "bomb" Nichole was going to drop, we had decided to take it in stride and look at it in light of where we were now in our family relationships. We would just take a clinical approach to any negative comments Nichole made, we reasoned, and it would work out okay.

I wish it had been that simple.

The second day, as a commercial break came to a close, Scott Ross glanced over his notes, watched the cameraman for the countdown, and we were all on the air: Adrienne and myself, Jason, Mark, Nichole and Lisa, who was outlined in a silhouette image on a monitor next to us.

"I'm Scott Ross and this is 'Straight Talk.' Today we're talking about blending families. You can say it in one breath, but it's much more difficult to accomplish."

Jason, Mark, Nichole and Lisa had already given brief descriptions of their blended family backgrounds at the beginning of the program. Now Scott turned to Nichole and addressed her with the after-the-break opening question.

"Nichole, what did you find most difficult about relating to a new parent?"

"The loyalty," Nichole answered, never hesitating.

"The loyalty. In what way?"

"I am closest to my father."

Going for more clarity, Scott interjected, "Your biological father?"

"Yes."

"So by showing any affection toward your stepfather you were being disloyal to your natural dad," Scott replied.

That is true and typical, I thought during their exchange. The loyalty conflict between the biological parent and the stepparent is difficult for children in blended families, and Nichole was no exception. But her next comment took both Adrienne and me by surprise.

"Yes, but I also resented my mother."

Scott probed, "You resented your mother?"

As Nichole continued I became acutely aware of Adrienne wilting in her chair.

"When you are only eight years old and your father leaves," explained Nichole, "you think it's your mother's fault because you're left there with her and your dad's gone. And it's like your mother made him leave. And that's what I thought for the longest time."

"And it wasn't true," Scott responded in a half-statement, half-question.

"It could have been," Nichole replied initially. Glancing over at her mother she added quickly, "but I don't think so."

That must have been what Nichole was so worried about expressing, I figured. But there was more.

Later in the program, Scott asked Nichole about her recollections of the transition years in our blended family.

"I don't remember much about that time," she answered. "I do remember Tom coming in and I remember Mom handing everything over to him. She just handed everything totally over to him and all of a sudden he was responsible for everything. We couldn't ask Mother anything. Mother immediately turned to Tom and asked him if it was all right if we did this or if we did that."

I couldn't believe what I was hearing. Nichole's resentment toward me I could understand. Resenting a stepparent goes with blended families as chocolate sauce goes with ice cream. I had prepared myself to hear Nichole express a number of things, but resentment toward her mother wasn't one of them. And even though Nichole was talking about the past, it hit Adrienne in the present.

"Straight Talk" came to a close, Scott made his concluding comments and we were off the air. As we walked off the set and back to the makeup room, it was clear that Nichole was relieved and Adrienne was devastated. I was trying to figure out where Nichole was coming from.

As is customary, after the program we had lunch with the other "Straight Talk" guests and the guest coordinator. When the meal was over, Nichole went back to our room, the guest coordinator went back to the network, the other guests left to go about their business in Virginia Beach, and Adrienne and I finally sat at the table alone.

I started our conversation the way I usually do in a tense situation.

"Well, Adrienne, what do you think?"

"I think I just can't believe it."

"What can't you believe?"

"I can't believe my own daughter portrayed me as a namby-pamby, simpering wimp totally controlled and dominated by you. And that apparently I had no mental capacities functioning to make even simple decisions. To hear Nichole talk you'd think that you, their stepfather, raised the girls without any help from their brain-dead biological mother. And that's just not true! I was not only involved, I was always in the middle—defending her, then defending you, then defending her, then defending you. . . .

"And as for her blaming me for the divorce, I was so concerned about the conflict the girls might feel between you and their biological father that I never dreamed the biggest loyalty conflict for Nichole was between me and her father."

As Adrienne continued venting, I nodded my head. But when I expressed sympathy about the disparaging nature of Nichole's comments, I got out only one or two sentences before Adrienne spoke up in Nichole's defense. I pushed back my chair and raised my arms in a mixed gesture of surrender and frustration.

"I can't say anything negative about that girl without you charging in to her defense."

We both sat there brooding. I finally broke the silence.

"She called me Tom on the program. She never calls me Tom. She always calls me Dad."

"I wonder what Nichole would have said if she knew her dad would never see the program," Adrienne wondered aloud. "I know he's really important to the girls, but sometimes, like now, I resent his input into this family portrait."

For our blended family, more was aired last summer than a television program. Nichole identified her resentment toward me for taking control and toward Adrienne for allowing it. Adrienne expressed resentment over being caught in the middle, over Nichole's lack of appreciation and at what she thought was my negative opinion of her daughter. I resented Nichole's misconception about my "coming in and taking over" and Adrienne's not following through when we agreed on rules.

When we came home from Virginia Beach and watched the videotape one of our friends had made for us, we began to analyze the program and our later interaction. Here we were—

we had written a book on this subject, we had done stepfamily seminars across the country, and yet there were so many issues, emotions and stresses wrapped up in blended family living that even the "experts" had problems to work out.

One stepfather told me, "My life is too short to put up with this much of a daily hassle. I will not live in a house with this much conflict."

This book, then, is the "straight talk" about the whos, the whys and the whens of anger, resentments and conflicts blended families experience. And because life *is* too short to live in constant conflict, it is also a book of hope, encouragement and answers.

— 2 —
Why Can't We Work Together?

"I feel so guilty about the ugly feelings I have toward the people I love and the people I'm supposed to love."

Linda wiped her eyes with an already tear-soaked tissue. Half-sighing, half-sobbing, she continued, "I just get so frustrated with myself. There are times when I know what to do, but I just can't force myself to do it. Last night my stepson, David, came home from school in a good mood. He very politely asked me a question, and my response was hateful.

"I know I hurt his feelings. I know I'm the adult in this situation. And I know I should have answered him with at least the common courtesy I would show an acquaintance. But he has been so rude to me so many times, and I have swallowed enough hurt, that whether he's being nice to me or not, I now find myself thinking, 'Why bother?' "

Quite agitated by now, Linda got up from her chair on the other side of my desk and, not looking at her husband, blurted out, "I resent the way Bill interacts with his children and not with mine. I resent the way my stepchildren turn on the charm when they want something and turn it off when they don't. I resent Bill's ex-wife and the way she manages to keep our lives in constant turmoil."

Sinking back into the chair, she sat in silence for a moment. Then she spoke very quietly. "And I resent sitting here in your office feeling so guilty and so frustrated after I've worked so hard at our marriage and our family."

At this point Bill, who had been sitting quietly beside his wife, interjected, "Yes, Linda, you've worked hard. I've worked hard. The kids have had to work some things out on their own. But we are not working together. Why is it you and I can't work together? Why can't we all work together as a family?

"And why do we have all this anger, this resentment toward each other? I feel it, too. I resent the way you give your children that second chance and you make mine 'toe the line.' I resent the way we have to work our family schedule around your ex-husband's schedule. And I hate it when your children come home loaded down with expensive gifts from their dad, or talking about the 'neat' things they did with him. My children think that's unfair and so do I."

Then Bill stopped and stared at the floor. After a few short moments, he continued.

"Tom, you know we didn't enter into this blended family situation lightly. We were aware of the problems we would have to face before we got married, and, for the most part, we know the answers. But *knowing* what to do is a whole lot different from *living* it."

After a short pause Bill went on. "There has to be a way to resolve all of this conflict. There has to be a way for our blended family to work."

Bill stopped talking and reached for Linda's hand. "I know Linda may find this hard to believe at times, but I love her. With all that's in me, I love her. But if we don't start working together instead of against each other, I'm just afraid . . . I'm so afraid of what I'll feel or won't feel a couple of years down the road."

The Suprasystem

Bill and Linda were no strangers to my office. I had met Bill and Linda at one of our blended family seminars; as a result they had driven to my office in Decatur for premarital counseling. During my counseling sessions with them we discussed the inherent problems of living in a blended family, what to expect in their particular situation and specific ways to resolve problems as they arise.

Now, eighteen months later, Bill and Linda were back in my office, both of them frustrated over their inability to work together. Yet what transpired in my office that day made it obvious that in spite of their difficulties and hurt feelings they still wanted their marriage to succeed.

Bill and Linda are not alone. None of us is alone. Through my counseling office and our public speaking, Adrienne and I have met numbers of blended families who are asking the very same question as Bill: "Why can't we work together?" The difficulties Bill and Linda were experiencing are common problems blended families face.

Marrying into a blended family can be compared to driving different vehicles. Perhaps I've been used to driving our family car on country roads, puttering along nice and easy, taking the curves with caution and experienced control. Now, all of a sudden, I find myself driving a semi-truck during the Los Angeles rush hour. I may have done quite well before, but I am not on country roads anymore. I have taken the ramp to a superhighway or, as books in the field of counseling say, the "suprasystem" (Sager, p. 3).

Blended families are not tightly knit nuclear families with one dad, one mom and one set of children all living in the same household, two sets of grandparents nearby, and his and her relatives.

Instead, blended families have two households directly and one or two other households indirectly involved in the system. Depending on the makeup of the two directly involved households, there are three or four parental figures, his, her and/or our children, anywhere from two to four sets of grandparents and a whole host of relatives.

Blended families are complex and are, therefore, prolific breeding grounds for resentment and conflict. Many blended family members walk around in their blended family supra-systems with unresolved anger, feeling they have been unjustly wronged or unjustly injured. And, whether consciously or unconsciously, their reasoning for not "working together" may go something like this: "If I've been unjustly injured, then I can use any means available to me to get my way—to get what I want. Because I have been unjustly wronged, there is no reason at all for me to play fair or cooperate. Why should I?"

What Makes Blended Families So Complex?

First, blended families are less cohesive than nuclear families. *Webster's* dictionary defines *cohere* as "to hold together firmly as parts of the same mass" and "to become united in principles, relationships, or interests." Because of the pre-existing alliances and loyalties different members bring into blended families, the existence of two households with permeable boundaries for the children and impermeable boundaries for the adults and the feelings of loss and insecurity held by their members, blended families do not have inherent "stick-togetherness." They have to work to become united, to "hold together firmly as parts of the same mass."

Second, blended families' roles, rules and responsibilities are ambiguous. Many aspects of blended family living are obscure and uncertain. Within the blended family suprasystem, members need to clarify roles and relationships between those within the same household and members of the other household(s).

What are the rights and obligations of a stepparent? Of a biological parent? Of a step or biological child? Who will discipline whom? What about rules and responsibilities? Who will do what, and who can't do what? Where are the role models, the rule books for blended families?

Other issues—some specific and some abstract—may cause resentments to flare between households in the blended family suprasystem. They may include:

- visitation and scheduling;
- the continual shift in household composition;
- different values, lifestyles and styles of discipline between households;
- permeable and impermeable boundaries (children living in and moving freely between two households while the adults do not);
- co-parenting (or lack of it) with the noncustodial parent(s);
- possible custody changes;
- shifts in the children's birth orders from one household to the next;

- both the children's and mates' relationships with the noncustodial parent(s);

- the ongoing influence and felt presence of the noncustodial parent(s) in a household;

- and so on, and so on.

Third, blended families are complex because they are full of stress. As one mother/stepmother put it, "Sometimes it's just overwhelming. Early in my second marriage I told myself, 'I can do this,' and I actually believed I could. But now that I'm in it, the stress level is so high it hasn't taken long for me to discover I need better coping skills. I don't deal well with all of this stress. As a matter of fact, and I'm ashamed to admit this, I know that at times I can be a real witch."

Not only do blended families have more stress, but the stressors in blended families never end. There is less stress when the children grow up, get married or are otherwise on their own, but they are still biological children or stepchildren relating to their biological parent(s) or stepparent(s). They are still members of two households with different values, lifestyles and multiple parental figures influencing their lives.

The complexity and stress involved in blended family living tax our personal resources psychologically, physically and spiritually. Sometimes we do not know the answer to a difficulty being experienced within the family. Sometimes we know the answer but lack the energy to implement it. And then there are those frustrating times when, like Linda, we have the solution and the energy, but refuse to take any action because we are full of resentment. In fact, we may actually precipitate the problem by our own behavior! Then we wonder introspectively along with Paul in Romans 7:19

why "what I do is not the good I want to do; no, the evil I do not want to do—this I keep on doing."

In our previous book, *The Blended Family,* we compared the stepparent's entering an already existing family system to feeling like an alien in a foreign land. It has now become apparent to us that it is not just the stepparent who feels this way. Everyone entering the new system feels as though he is in a foreign land, in unfamiliar territory.

Because of this feeling of unfamiliarity and strangeness, blended family members are self-conscious and keenly aware of their own actions and the actions of other family members. Just as you would look around in a strange land and ask, "Why are they doing what they're doing?" or "Why are they doing it that way?" and "Why don't they do it the right way?," so do the members of the new blended family system. Everything is examined, questioned and analyzed.

This acute awareness of others within the system could promote deep understanding and empathy. Unfortunately it tends, instead, to create judging, blaming, anger and resentment.

The next three chapters deal with the resentments of different blended family members. As you read through them, you may be able to identify the origins of your own feelings of resentment. We hope that reading these particular chapters will help you recognize that other members of your blended family have equally valid feelings of resentment.

You *will* discover as you read that many people have the same resentments you do. In our blended family seminars we have discovered that many couples had never openly admitted that theirs were blended families. Neither had they ever shared their feelings with other blended family couples. As they talked, they were relieved to discover that their experiences were not abnormal or unusual, but all part of blended family living.

Your feelings, your mate's feelings and your children's feelings are normal for blended families. While we hope this realization is helpful, we also hope you see that allowing those resentments to continue is very detrimental to your blended family life and to you as an individual.

Later in this book we will look at ways to add structure and develop specific skills in order to reduce resentments and bring long-term peace and harmony to your blended family household.

Throughout the next three chapters you will find boxes (□) in the left margin. If you identify with a particular problem we address, mark the box. After you have read the book and are ready to begin working on problem areas you have identified, the boxes you have marked will serve as a quick reference guide.

— 3 —
Biological Parents' Resentments

If you had a magic wand, to use a fairy tale term, and you could wave it over your blended family to make everything just the way you wanted it, how would your blended family be different? This is one of our favorite questions, and I ask it of clients in my office and of participants at our blended family seminars. The answers often tell us where resentments lie.

Although we hear a variety of responses, most revolve around the same basic themes: the blended family system, conflicts over loyalty, blended family relationships (which include all of the various combinations of blended family members), discipline, family bonding and the other household.

Let's look first at some biological parents' answers to our fairy tale question as they relate to each of these basic areas, and uncover the resentments they reveal. We will look next at stepparents' feelings. I strongly urge you—whatever your position—to read the chapters about the others as well. Understanding how the other side sometimes feels is crucial for healing to begin to take place. And, of course, many of you fill dual roles—stepparent and biological parent, stepchild and biological child.

The System

"If I had a magic wand, the first thing I would do is make my blended family into a nuclear family. Now that would fix everything."

Why do we want to make our blended families into nuclear families? One reason is that this suprasystem we call a blended family is born out of loss: loss of the nuclear family system with its stability, its structure, its benefits and its status, and loss of the nuclear family dream.

☐   One father/stepfather feels he is always scrambling to maintain a sense of *stability* within his blended family.

"I hate the constant shifting in our household. Every other night during the week her children sleep over. Mine stay with us every other Saturday and Sunday. It seems like our whole family life revolves around moving one set of children in and one set of children out."

Because the composition of a blended family is always changing, the interaction between family members is also in constant change.

☐   As we stated earlier, when you lose the nuclear family system, you lose its simple *structure*.

Beverly, a mother/stepmother, expresses total exasperation over the complexity of her blended family system.

"We have three subgroups in our family, one for each child. We have my husband and his son, Mark. We have me and my daughter, Carol. Then we have my husband and me and our daughter, Amanda, somewhere in the middle. Which subgroup operates when is decided by which child is currently present. I resent not having just one group: Mom, Dad and the kids in my family."

☐   Sandy laments over the *benefits* she and her children used to have in their previous nuclear family system.

"I always had that other person to take care of me and of our children in my first marriage. Now I have to take care of myself and the children. I'm the one who drives them everyplace and goes to their activities. I resent being the one who worries myself sick over them. I'm angry because their father's not here twenty-four hours a day worrying about them the way I do. My new husband isn't too concerned with what's happening in my children's lives either, because they aren't his kids."

☐   Ann, on the other hand, is angry over what she feels is a loss of *status* she derived from her first marriage.

"My ex is a very influential person in the community. His connections used to be my connections, too. Now I'm a nobody and, although this may sound awful, I resent my children's having the kind of social access I once had."

☐   The loss of the *nuclear family dream* is a very difficult resentment to lay to rest. Almost everyone who has gone through a divorce and then remarried struggles with the "what ifs," "why didn'ts" or "why can'ts." And almost every biological parent we have talked with resents having a divorce behind them, their mate, or both. One mother/stepmother living in a blended family made this statement concerning her remarriage:

"I resent having a divorce behind me and having four adults in this system. I resent not being my husband's first— his first love, his first wife and the woman who bore his first child. And I resent all of the extra baggage that comes from being married before: the extra financial burden, my interfering ex-husband, his crazy ex-wife, a hyperactive stepchild and feelings of rejection and guilt left over from our first marriages."

☐   Biological parents may resent the loss of the nuclear family dream not only for themselves, but also for their children. One of my clients, tight-lipped and teary-eyed, got right to the point when I asked her what she resented most about living in a blended family.

"I resent having to carry around this aching, gut-deep sadness because my children will never have the security of a nuclear family. I resent knowing my husband will never really feel the closeness that a father is supposed to feel for his children. And I resent knowing my children won't get that 'you're my child no matter what' support they're supposed to get from a daddy—from my husband."

☐   Part of the offense biological parents feel for their children is due to the unrealistic expectation that a new mate will love their children as their own—and that their children will love a new mommy or daddy in the same unrealistic way.

Ginny was disillusioned by her husband's and children's lack of cooperation in living up to her expectations.

"I want my husband to love my kids as I do. He should. They're nice kids. But he doesn't. He says he does, but he doesn't love them the way I do. I want my kids to love my husband as I do. And they should. He's nice to them. He goes out of his way for them. But they don't. They can't even say thank you for the things he does for them, let alone express the love toward him that I thought they would."

☐   Resentment over the loss of the nuclear family dream even filters down to explaining step-relationships to children. How do we do it? When do we do it? Why do we even have to deal with step-relationships? Why can't we just live in a nuclear system like the all-American family next door?

As one biological parent put it,

"I'm not looking forward to explaining to my younger sons [two-year-old twins] that their older brother has a different father. The impact on them when he's gone out of state to visit his dad for six weeks in the summer is already difficult for me to get used to."

Loyalty Conflicts

"To have a magic wand like that would mean I would no longer be caught in the middle, understanding both sides and being empathetic toward both."

Loyalty conflicts are the biggest area of resentment for the biological parent. When it comes to feeling unjustly wronged or unjustly injured this area can provoke even the mildest-mannered blended family member into an uproar.

☐   Biological parents struggle constantly with being caught in the middle between their children and their new mate. They resent being put into a position where they feel as if anything they do is choosing sides.

☐   Biological parents also find themselves in loyalty conflicts between their children and the other biological parent.

Linda, perplexed and angered over her children's loyalty to their father, shared this with us.

"My children's father doesn't love them the way I do. He isn't as interested in their lives as I am. He isn't at all concerned about their spiritual growth. And what does he care if they have a school concert on Wednesday night or not? Sometimes the kids are lucky if he shows up for visitation. In spite of all that, my children still think he is Mr. Wonderful, Mr. Perfect, Super Biodad. They are so worried about hurting his feelings, it makes me angry. Why are they so loyal to him, and so disrespectful to me?"

☐   Biological parents may also experience conflicting feelings of loyalty toward their children and stepchildren.

Sam, a parent/stepparent, described just such a situation.

"With so many teenagers in our household my wife and I had to come to an agreement concerning their use of the car. The girls use the car on Friday nights and the boys drive it on Saturday nights, alternating every other weekend. Last Saturday night was my stepson's weekend to get the car. Even though he didn't have anything special planned, he still wanted to take it. My son, however, did have plans—his first date with a girl he's been crazy about for a long time. Although my wife and I had already decided on who gets the car what night, I really felt my son should have been allowed to take it. My stepson wasn't doing anything special anyway. Why couldn't he just give up one Saturday night?"

Sam felt torn between being faithful to his word, which he had given to his stepson, or loyal to his son, who had a need.

Blended Family Relationships

"If I had a magic wand, I would line my family up, wave the wand over them and 'poof!' . . . perfect family relationships."

The Stepparent/Stepchild Relationship

☐   The number-one complaint biological parents make regarding the stepparent/stepchild relationship is, "My mate doesn't love my children as I do."

Jan, a young, vivacious mother/stepmother, had this to say about her husband, Tim's, relationship with her daughter.

"I was really wide-eyed and naïve going into my second marriage. I would learn to love Tim's little boy and he would learn to love my little girl and since we already loved each other, what could possibly keep us from being just one big happy family? I soon began to realize Tim was not going to be as attentive to my child as I thought he would be, let alone love her. Through the months I finally decided I would be responsible for my daughter and he would be responsible for his son."

□ Biological parents tend to lack trust in a new mate's decisions when it comes to their children.

Monica shared how she felt when her husband, Greg, made decisions concerning her son, Jordan.

"I trust Greg's judgment completely when it comes to his son. Whatever he says goes. I don't trust Greg with decisions for Jordan, however, and I resent it when he makes decisions for him without consulting me. Greg doesn't know Jordan's history. I know Jordan's past and where he's coming from."

□ Many biological parents also resent a new mate's super-sensitivity in taking a stepchild's every action as a personal affront.

"John doesn't see my children as kids misbehaving, but feels their misbehavior is directed toward him. When he tells them to put their bicycles in the garage at night and they don't, he thinks they have purposely set out to get even with him or to make him mad. He doesn't even consider the very real possibility that they simply forgot or they're just being lazy."

☐   Stepparents who take their stepchildren's actions as personal affronts may become critical of everything their stepchildren do. And if stepparents are also biological parents, they often fail to see what they consider to be problem behavior in their stepchildren as equally problematic in their biological children.

Andy, a father and stepfather of four, voiced his resentment concerning this issue.

"As far as my wife is concerned, there is 'no slack' when it comes to my kids. She doesn't have the same attitude of grace and generosity toward my children that she has toward hers. She's quick to point out the personality flaws in my children but wears blinders when it comes to her kids."

☐   Stepparents' involvement in activities with their stepchildren is very significant to the bonding process. As Susan, a parent/stepparent, shares, resentment over the time *not* spent by a stepparent with a stepchild can wreak havoc in the blending of a family.

"It never occurs to my husband to involve my daughter, Amy, in things he's doing. But when his son and daughter are here, he automatically includes them in everything and takes them wherever he goes, even if it's just to run silly errands. I really resent my husband's exclusion of my daughter when his children are here, but what I resent even more is his not wanting to do anything with just Amy and me. He always wants to wait to go to the park until his kids are here. We can't go to the zoo because he doesn't want his children to miss out. And he doesn't want to take Amy to a movie because he's just too tired; then he'll remind me that his kids will be here next weekend and we can all go then."

☐   When biological parents feel their children aren't receiving enough love and affection from their mate, they may overcompensate by giving their children extra time and attention. Stepparents may then become even more distant in their relationships with their stepchildren, or jealous of the parent/child relationship.

The stepparent might also become jealous of the parent/child relationship due to: overbonding between parent and child; selfishness in not wanting to share his or her new mate with the stepchildren; or the biological parent's insensitivity to his or her new mate's needs. Whatever the reason, the stepparent's jealousy over the parent/child relationship can be a major source of resentment for the biological parent.

Wendell, a noncustodial father, enjoys taking his daughter to the YMCA Indian Princess and Guides meetings and campouts, but his new wife is extremely jealous of the time he spends with his daughter.

"My wife gets angry and insanely jealous over the time I spend with Ericka on weekend campouts and weekly meetings, so I actually end up feeling guilty over spending time with my own daughter. It's not like I'm seeing some other woman. Good grief, it's only my eight-year-old daughter."

The Parent/Child Relationship

☐   Feelings of guilt over putting their children through a divorce and its continuing repercussions have been a recurring theme in our sessions with biological parents.

As one of my clients so aptly put it:

"I feel my children resent me for 'ruining their lives' by putting them through a divorce. They blame me and the divorce when things aren't going well for them. Then I begin blaming myself because they don't resemble the perfect picture of happy, emotionally healthy, well-adjusted kids. I resent my children blaming me and the divorce for everything that goes wrong in their lives, and I get angry with myself for accepting the blame."

☐   One of the major stressors and biggest fears for the custodial biological parent is "the big threat": "I'll just move in with Dad/Mom."

Frank got hot over his son's use of the big threat.

"Nothing makes me angry as fast as when my son, Corey, threatens me with, 'I'll go back with Mom.' The last time he pulled that stunt, I looked at him and said, 'There's the phone. Pick it up and get your plane ticket. Our front door is not a revolving door. You are not going to put your mother and me through the agony of your coming and going again and again. The truth of the matter is, you're going to have good and bad times no matter whose house you live in.' He didn't pick up the phone."

☐   Biological parents may also become angry with their children for blocking the bonding process with the new mate.

"Why can't my fourteen-year-old son, Buddy, be nice once in a while to my husband?" complained Susan. "Instead, he's obnoxious one moment and treating him like a nonperson the next. I get so mad at my son when my husband attempts to be friendly and Buddy reacts with a look of complete disdain or a smart remark. I resent my son's unwillingness to give an inch, to treat my husband with respect or to work at making this a family."

The Child/Stepchild Relationship

☐   "My husband's teenaged daughters are feminine, pretty and popular; my thirteen-year-old daughter is a little overweight, average-looking, somewhat tomboyish and not as popular at school. His daughters look right, talk right, act right and are at the top of the pecking order. When they come to spend the weekend, my daughter ends up feeling the same kind of rejection in her own home that she does at school.

"They don't treat her like a sister by trying to help her or protect her. They treat her like a third-class citizen, an untouchable, or like she has leprosy. They act as if just being nice to her would jeopardize their social position. I can't find the words—nice words, anyway—to express how much I resent my stepdaughters' attitude toward my daughter, especially when I hear her crying in her room on the nights they come to stay. Why is it so difficult for them to be nice to her?"

Not only has this mother voiced her resentment as a biological mother, but also as a stepmother. She sees her daughter's pain in being ostracized within the family unit.

☐   In some blended families the biological mom's or dad's children may do the snubbing.

"I become so angry with my children when my stepchildren come over to spend some time with us," says June. "My children act selfish and unaccepting. My daughter doesn't want her stepsister to sit on her bed, touch anything in her room or even pet 'her' dog. My two sons, who are a couple of years older than their stepbrother, call him 'baby' and 'shrimp' and have to be forced into doing anything with him.

"Every time my stepchildren come over, one or sometimes both of them end up crying. This upsets my husband and he ends up getting mad at my children and me. Then his children become even more agitated because they've made their dad angry. I resent my children's refusal to accept their stepbrother and stepsister, and the stress and anxiety this conflict adds to my life."

The Couple Relationship

Resentments from other relationships within the blended family unit cannot help but spill over into the couple relationship.

☐   Tricia, a custodial parent, resents her husband's attitude concerning child support.

"Why can't my husband get off my back about child support? I don't like having to rely on my ex's money in the first place. To have my mate bugging me all the time to take my ex back to court for more money really irks me. Even if I did, and they ordered him to pay more money, I'd probably never see it. Why can't my husband understand that I have a hard enough time dealing with my ex as it is? I don't need two of them jumping on my case all the time."

☐   Robin resents her mate's resentment of her ex.

"I'm sick and tired of hearing Nick put down my first husband. I love Nick and most definitely don't want to be back with my first husband. But that doesn't give Nick the right to slam me about it. He's always making snide remarks about my ex-husband. According to him, I was once married to a 'homely, squirrely, less than human imbecile.' What does that make me?"

☐   Mark, a noncustodial parent, resents his wife's attitude toward his visiting children.

"When my children come to stay with us every other weekend, my wife chooses to become emotionally comatose. Instead of interacting with us as a family, she shuts herself in our bedroom and reads, coming out only to cook an occasional meal. When she does grace us with her presence, her remarks toward my children are sarcastic and cutting. Then my children can't wait for her to go back into the bedroom.

What she's basically saying to me is, 'I can't wait until your little brats are gone.' Not only do I resent her hostile attitude toward my children, I'm beginning to resent her."

A couple may have said to one another initially, "We have a problem. We have a problem with my children not accepting your children. We have a problem with bonding between you and little Johnny or overbonding between little Susie and me. We have a problem with loyalty conflicts."

Unfortunately, if the unresolved conflict lingers, the conversation switches, as it did in Mark's case, from "we have a problem" to "you *are* the problem." The couple no longer works together on finding a solution.

Of all the difficulties a blended family couple has to contend with, the number-one issue that creates the switch from "we have a problem" to "you are the problem" is the area of discipline. You may relate to some of the following examples.

Discipline

"If I had a magic wand, when my husband disciplines my children, he would do it in love. And he would realize that there are exceptions to the rule.

☐   Biological parents often become irate when stepparents leap into the arena of discipline by setting up new rules and guidelines for their stepchildren—especially without consulting them.

"Nothing makes me more angry than to walk in and find my son, Jimmy, either standing in the corner or banished to his room for breaking a rule my husband and I never agreed upon or even discussed, for that matter," says Cindy. "When I came home from work one day last week, I heard Jimmy crying in his room. When I asked what was wrong, he told me his stepfather had taken his bicycle away for a week because he had ridden it to his friend Nathan's house. I always let Jimmy ride his bike to his little friend's house, even though it's one block out of his riding radius. My husband *knows* Jimmy rides his bike to Nathan's. If he didn't think Jimmy should be riding his bike that far, why couldn't he have waited until I got home to discuss it with me, instead of jumping on Jimmy for breaking a rule we have never established?"

☐   Many biological parents find themselves caught in the middle between their children and their new mate in the area of discipline.

Lana, mother of two grown children, tells it like this:

"I was always in the middle. I would hear from my kids what happened. Then I would hear from my husband, Rodney, what happened. And on some occasions I would be carrying messages back and forth between them.

"Before Rodney and I were married, my children and I lived in an okay house with a so-so yard. As a single mother, I had other things to worry about besides keeping my lawn well-groomed. So I didn't mind if my son, Chris, drove his car through the yard to get around my car. Rodney, on the other hand, lived in a very nice house with a manicured yard. When we were married my children and I moved into Rodney's house. The first time Chris drove through the yard to get around one of our cars, Rodney threw a fit—with *me!* He told me, in no uncertain terms, to tell Chris to stay off the lawn with his car. I went to Chris and told him Rodney didn't want him driving on the lawn. That was just the beginning.

"My playing the middleman got so bad I just couldn't deal with it anymore. One day my daughter was griping about Rodney, and told me, once again, that she hated him. I'd had enough. I just looked at her and said, 'Okay, hate him if you want to. But hate him to his face. Don't put me in the middle.' "

□   When stepparents confront their stepchildren head-on, however, with or without just cause, biological parents' re-actions vary, but all carry the same message:

"He's always on my children."

"Every time he walks in the room, he's policing."

"She's too hard on my son."

"My daughter came to me and complained that my wife always jumps on her case. I told my wife, 'You talk to me and I'll talk to my daughter.' "

□   Sometimes biological parents resent their mate's lack of empathy for a stepchild, and an unwillingness to make oc-casional exceptions to an agreed-upon rule.

Mike, a custodial parent, described one of several situa-tions like this.

"The rule in our house for curfew is 11 P.M. Saturday night. My son came in forty minutes late, saying he'd had a flat tire. Before I had a chance to say anything, my wife jumped right in. 'It doesn't make any difference. Flat tire or not, curfew is eleven o'clock. You are forty minutes late. Therefore, you are grounded.'

"My wife wasn't even *trying* to understand. All she had to do was go out to the car, look in the trunk and check for a flat tire. I checked and the kid was not lying. This wasn't a cheap trick to fool us. The kid had a flat tire. I was glad he changed it himself instead of calling me. My wife didn't want to understand. She just wanted to punish my son."

□   Unfair treatment between children can cause strong resentment on the part of biological parents.

"My husband, Jeff, and I established the rule, No jumping on the bed," says Laurie. "When *my* son, Todd, jumps on the bed, Jeff sends him to the corner immediately. No warning.

No nothing. Just, 'Stop jumping on the bed and get into that corner.'

"When *our* son, Brandon, jumps on the bed, Jeff says, 'Aw, come on, man. You know you're not supposed to be jumping on the bed. If you jump on the bed again you're going to have to stand in the corner. That's the rule. I'd hate to have to send you to the corner, so don't jump on the bed, okay, buddy?' "

☐   Sometimes biological parents in blended families end up feeling like single parents again. Whether it is because they are tired of their mate's making up new rules without consulting them, burned out from being in the middle, unable to deal with their mate's style of discipline, weary of their mate's policing the household, upset over unfair treatment of their children or revolting against their mate's lack of empathy toward their children, some biological parents will assume the role of a single parent when it comes to discipline, even though they dislike it.

Other biological parents may be forced into the role of sole disciplinarian because their mate refuses to parent his or her stepchildren out of insecurity or anger at the biological parent over discipline.

Janet took on that role.

"I might as well be a single parent again. All day and all night I have all of the parenting responsibilities. I make sure my children do their homework. I make sure they do their chores. I'm the one who stands them in the corner or sends them to their rooms when they misbehave. I resent the pressure of always being 'the heavy.' And I resent not being able to share anything with Steve about the kids, including discipline."

When a biological parent takes sole responsibility for discipline in the blended family household, the family has not bonded.

Family Bonding

"Family loyalty and togetherness, that's what a magic wand would bring to our blended family. All for one and one for all, just like in the movies."

☐   Just as doing things together is so important for bonding in the stepparent/stepchild relationship (see chapter 6 on bonding in *The Blended Family*), participating in activities together as a family is equally important to family bonding.

Sarah expressed her disappointment over her husband's unwillingness to take part in family activities.

"We never do anything as a family unit. When the kids and I are watching TV, he's watching something else in a different room. I don't think we even had dinner together once during the Christmas holidays when the children were home from school. We never have family outings. I resent not being able to enjoy things together as a family. It breaks my heart that my husband misses or bows out of opportunities to bond with me and my children."

☐   Robert was equally resentful over his wife's reluctance to join him and his children in their extended families' activities.

"My wife always has an excuse for not going to my family's get-togethers. When she does go, she won't join in any of the conversations or activities. My family has always had so much fun together, and I want that so much for my family. But it's really hard to have family fun when my wife purposely blocks family bonding.

"She even blocks our bonding with her family. She either makes arrangements for us to go out-of-state to see her folks when she knows my children can't come along, or decides to visit on the spur of the moment with just her children. I've given up trying to get my kids together with her extended family. Our time with them has dwindled down to one visit a year at Christmas. When we're there for our yearly visit, her family is very accepting of my children. It's my wife who makes them feel as though they don't belong."

☐   Family pride and family spirit are feelings that come with family bonding.

"Sometimes I picture my husband, myself and all of our children cheering at a ballgame or sitting proudly at an awards ceremony saying, 'That's our kid,' or, 'That's our brother. We're so proud of him,' " Alice comments wistfully. "But then I come back to the real world where neither my mate nor our children experience that sense of family pride or loyalty. And they may never feel it. When I think about that possibility, I really resent not being able to experience family pride within my blended family."

Family loyalty *within* a blended family is often affected from *without* the family by the other household.

The Other Household

"With my trusty wand in hand, I would run across town, wave it over the other household and make it disappear."

Many biological parents (and stepparents) have cheered when hearing this parent's response to the magic wand question. If you could make the other household disappear, your blended family would be free of the hassles inherent in having two households (or possibly more) in your blended family suprasystem. Then you would not have to deal with an

ex-mate, a same-sex stepparent, visitation, holidays and loyalty conflicts.

The Ex-Mate

The resentments biological parents may feel toward their
ex-mates can be related to a variety of issues, but often hinge
around "who's got the power?" One power struggle that can
bring custodial and noncustodial parents directly into conflict
is money. Who has it? Who doesn't?

☐   Betty, a custodial parent, related her feelings of resentment over "who doesn't have it."

"I feel as if my ex is always one up on me in my kids' eyes.
He's smarter than I; he can give them better things; and he
takes them to fun places. He got my son, Bobby, a job last
winter just by making a phone call.

"When my children walk into their other household, they
walk into a very expensive house with luxurious furnishings.
When they go to see their dad over the weekend, I sit in our
modest home and think, *Why wouldn't they be thrilled to go over
there?* And I become resentful over how much more he has
than we do. Then I really get ticked because he doesn't pay as
much child support as he should, but I'm afraid to go back to
court for additional support. If I did he'd raise a big stink and
tell the kids I'm nothing but a 'money-grubber.' "

☐   George, a noncustodial parent, aired his feelings of resentment over the issue of child support.

"I've been married twice before and pay child support to
both households. I pay thirty percent of my income to my
first ex-wife and twenty percent of my income to my second
ex-wife. Any way you add that up, it equals poor. My first
ex-wife is an insurance agent, and her husband is an airline

pilot. My second ex-wife, who is still a single parent, has a very good job. As a matter of fact, she has done well enough financially to buy herself a new house and a new car.

"My wife and I and her children live in a very small house, and I drive a piece of junk. I didn't resent paying child support in the beginning. I didn't mind suffering then. But once their lives got established and they were doing better financially, why couldn't they cut me some slack? To top it all off, I didn't want either one of the divorces to begin with."

☐   Biological parents seem to find that their children show anger for the divorce and remarriage toward the parent they live with on a daily basis. Adrienne and I learned this firsthand when Nichole expressed her feelings during the television interview. As one other biological parent, Joe, expressed it, "I resent the way my ex-wife, in spite of what she put us through, still comes out smelling like a rose to my children."

☐   Some biological parents feel they are being forced by their ex-mates into a power struggle over the children. They view their ex-mates as annoying interferences in their lives, and most troublesome when it comes to the children.

☐   While some biological parents feel their ex-mates are forcing themselves into their lives, other biological parents feel their ex-mates are trying to squeeze them out of their children's lives. Jerry wants to be an involved parent, but his ex-mate tries her best to exclude him.

"If my ex-wife, Fran, would work half as hard at being a good mother as she does at trying to make me look like a bad father, she might be of some benefit to the boys. She doesn't want me to call them because it's too upsetting. She finds it all but impossible to work her schedule or the boys' ballgames around my visitation with them, and keeps making the ridiculous suggestion that I forget it. She refuses to let me know when and where their games are, leaving me to track their coaches down for the schedules. She tells them not to show me their report cards because 'your dad's not really interested anyway. If he really cared about you, he wouldn't have left.'

"I resent having to fight Fran to get to my children, and then, when I am with them, fighting the negative messages and insinuations she has artfully planted in their minds about my new wife and me."

☐   Another biological mother, Renee, resents her ex-mate's lack of cooperation.

"On the day my seventeen-year-old son, Roger, left to go on vacation with his dad, I was looking in his desk drawer for a computer disc. I didn't find the computer disc, but I did find a bottle of vodka. I called Roger's father to tell him I'd found it. The first thing he said to me was, 'Why were you going through his desk drawers?' As if I didn't have a right to go into my own son's room!

"Ignoring his question, I asked him please to talk to Roger about the dangers of drinking, particularly in light of certain medical problems. When I mentioned that we don't have alcohol in our household, my ex gave me a ten-minute lecture about his family's moderate use of alcohol when he was growing up and his lack of a drinking problem. He feels Roger won't necessarily have a drinking problem just because his father drinks occasionally and has alcohol in the house.

"I resent my ex's continued refusal to cooperate with me when it comes to the well-being of our son."

The Same-Sex Stepparent

☐   Becky found it very difficult to accept her son's step-mother as a part of his life.

"When Richard remarried right after our divorce, his wife was no threat to me, especially since my son, J.D., was so young and really didn't care for her much anyway. When Richard remarried a second time, I felt a lot of resentment toward his wife, Paula. This time around J.D. was calling his stepmother 'Mom.' She was always causing an uproar in our household—stirring up trouble between J.D. and me or his stepdad, or talking my ex into going to court (several times) over custody. It became very difficult for me to let J.D. go to his other household; I never knew what new tricks she had pulled or what kind of mood my son would be in when he came back."

□   The same-sex stepparent who accidentally or intentionally "invades" territory biological parents have reserved as theirs can stir up hard feelings between households, especially when it comes to their children's personal appearance. In the eyes of the biological parent, this territory may include such things as haircuts, makeup or, as this mother shared, earrings.

"In our household we have a tradition concerning ear piercing: To us, it's a custom marking our daughters' entry into womanhood. Our rule has always been that the girls can get their ears pierced when they turn thirteen, and not a day before. The weekend before my youngest daughter, Cindy's, thirteenth birthday her stepmother took her to get her ears pierced. I couldn't believe it. She didn't even consult me or my ex. I was so angry! That was supposed to be *my* special time with my daughter, not hers."

□   Biological parents, whether custodial or noncustodial, resent a same-sex stepparent's failure to accept their children.

"Sometimes I think my daughter's stepmother hates her," says Hanna. "My daughter is quiet and pretty easy to get along with, which makes me wonder why her stepmother has labeled her as an attention-seeker and a troublemaker. She's never been thrilled about my daughter's visits, but since they've had a new baby, she's pushing my ex to make visitation a movie or a trip to a restaurant instead of including my daughter in any activities in their home."

Visitation

☐   When your children go to the other household or arrive at your household, resentment can start before they even get out or in the door. Just ask Marla, a custodial parent:

"When my children are ready to leave for their other household, I never know how close to the appointed pickup time my ex will be. Sometimes he's early; sometimes he's late; but he's never on time. When I talk to him about it, he makes a smart remark like, 'Oh, I'm just trying to keep you on your toes.' I hate feeling like I have no control over the whole process of 'pickup and delivery' of my children, and I resent my ex writing me off when I try to discuss it with him."

☐   Other resentments may occur with children's coming and going in their other household.

"Whenever the kids come over we play 'what's in the suitcase?,' " says Shane, a noncustodial parent. "I never know from one visit to the next whether the clothes will be clean, dirty, matching or nonmatching. Sometimes my ex sends clothes for church or dress-up occasions and sometimes she doesn't. It just depends on the kind of mood she's in when she packs. I've learned to keep two or three complete outfits and some dress clothes here for my children. I resent my ex playing this little 'get even' game with every visitation."

☐   While their children are in the other household, some biological parents, both custodial and noncustodial, resent the ambiguity involved in blended families—the doubtful, uncertain, obscure or indistinct influences on their children over which they have no control.

"It's very difficult for me to deal with not knowing who is involved in my children's lives, and I resent it," said Julie, a custodial parent. "I have no idea who Aunt Sis is, or cousin Billie. I don't even know what my children's stepbrother and stepsister are like. What kind of impact are they having on my children's lives, positive or negative? I hate not knowing."

Ambiguity presents daily pain for Larry, a noncustodial parent.

"I miss the daily interaction that is so important for really knowing my children. I feel very inept about teaching my children Christian values and influencing their Christian walk when I only see them one day a week and every other weekend. I want them to go to a Christian school, and have offered to pay their tuition, but their mother refuses. How frustrating it is for me to write a generous check for child support, and be unable to have any say in how it's spent, especially when it comes to clothes and schooling."

☐   Discipline in the other household can have a profound effect on your household. You may think the other household is too lenient and they may think you are too strict, or vice-versa.

☐   Norman, a noncustodial parent, is concerned about the leniency in his son's other household.

"My sixteen-year-old, David, begged and begged me to let him move in with his mother. I kept refusing because his mother is so liberal and lacking in basic parenting skills. When he threatened to run away, I finally agreed to the move, against my better judgment. David's mother, who doesn't get off work until six o'clock, bought him a car as soon as he moved in. Now, not only does he have a car to run around in, he also has a lot of unsupervised time in which to do it. Who knows what he does or where he goes? She sure doesn't. If I question either of them about it, I'm being 'too narrow.'

"I'm concerned about David's spiritual growth, too. Before he moved out he promised to be in church every Sunday, and he's lived up to his promise. But he quit doing things with his friends at church, and he's stopped going to youth group. The boys he's running around with are nice kids, but they are not Christians. As I see his values and beliefs slipping, I can't help but wonder if he will eventually think partying, drinking and premarital sex are okay. I resent my son's having an option to move into another household, especially when that household is so lax in its standards and spiritual beliefs. Bottom line? I want my son back home, and his mother's influence out of his life."

☐   But Stephanie, also a noncustodial parent, feels the other household is too strict and stifling.

"My son, Jordan, fifteen, and my daughter, Anna, eight, are very bright, sensible children who are not allowed any freedom in their other household. Anna is not allowed out of her father's and stepmother's sight. How will she ever learn to be on her own? Jordan can't go to the school dances or ball games. How will he practice his social skills if they never let him out of the house? Experiences make children grow, not overprotection."

Holidays

☐   The act of bearing gifts brings to mind thoughts of holidays, joy and peace. But in some blended family situations, gift-giving instead produces hurt feelings and resentments.

Jessie, a widow with two teenagers, married a divorced man who also had two teenagers.

"From the day we married, Don and I tried to keep things equal, but it didn't work. For our first Christmas, we decided to spend one hundred dollars on gifts for each child. I was very careful to do so, almost to the penny. What a letdown for my children and me when Don's children returned home on Christmas Day loaded with so many presents from their other household, it looked like they'd each won a shopping spree at the mall. My children cried for days over how unfair it was. I hated seeing my children hurt and I resented working so hard on equality in our household only to have it completely thrown out of balance by the other household's spending. I spent more money on my kids the next Christmas, on their birthdays and at Eastertime."

☐   Adrienne and I resented the changing composition of our household during the holidays. When Nichole and Jennifer were at their other household, it just wasn't the same for the rest of us, with two fewer plates at the Christmas brunch and two fewer people to hold hands with for prayer at Grandma Frydenger's Easter dinner.

It was especially hard for our son, Luke. He missed having the girls around to open Christmas presents and join in on our traditional Christmas treasure and Easter egg hunts.

Loyalty Conflicts Between Households

With children living in two households, loyalty conflicts between households are almost inevitable. While in this case the children have the divided loyalties, the biological parents definitely feel the strain. For example:

☐   "The very week I sent my daughter, Christine, off to her first year in college, my sixteen-year-old son, Chad, announced he was going to move in with his dad," Janette told us. "Looking back, I can see that part of Chad's loyalty to this household was due to his close relationship with Christine. When Christine left, so did Chad's loyalty.

"Ten-year-old Mickey, my other son, cried all day when Chad moved out. Being the only one left at home is hard on him. He doesn't want to sleep by himself upstairs anymore, and in the mornings I often find him curled up in his sleeping bag outside our bedroom door. I resent Chad's having more loyalty to the other household than to ours, or to his little brother, Mickey. My husband and I have only been married four years. We haven't even become a family yet, and now it's even more difficult because part of my family is gone."

As you biological parents read this chapter you might have checked box after box, saying to yourself, "That's exactly how I feel. I can identify with that." Checking boxes helped you to work on the first step toward resolving conflict in your blended family: identifying your resentments.

Identifying those resentments may not have been easy, but being able to empathize with the resentments expressed in the next two chapters may be even more difficult. If you are a stepparent, I hope you have realized through reading this chapter that what you have been hearing from your mate is not just your mate's problem, but what many biological parents are expressing. In fact, the resentments expressed by all blended family members, whether they are biological parents, stepparents, stepchildren or biological children, are equally real.

Let's explore how you stepparents feel.

— 4 —
Stepparents' Resentments

"When I started dating Marie I was on cloud nine. We were perfect for each other. She was everything I ever wanted: beautiful, intelligent and a musician, like me. Before I met her my life was a song of dissonance, but with Marie it was a harmony.

"It didn't make any difference to me that Marie had three children from a previous marriage. I was in love with Marie and they were just, well, part of the package. I have always been very family-oriented and thought I would make a great dad for her kids. I would be starting out with the family I have always wanted anyway, but we'd get a whole day a week, and an occasional weekend, off!

"What a joke! I had no idea being a stepparent was going to be this tough. I have always thought of myself as a really nice guy; now when I look in the mirror I see this angry, resentful man staring back at me."

Being a stepparent *is* tough. Although stepparents' resentments follow the same basic themes as those of biological parents, the issues stepparents feel strongly about regarding

those themes are different. What would stepparents change if
they had magic wands?

The System

*"If I had a magic wand, I would take the word 'step' out of
stepfather. Then I'd be just a father. No, then I'd be a dad."*

The stepparent's contention with the system arises not
out of loss, but out of what stepparents are inheriting. As
soon as they say "I do" they assume negative images, undefined roles and family systems that are already set up and
functioning. When you add to that unrealistic expectations
and the realization that, as stepparents, they will not experience the nuclear family dream, the system can be a source
of deep resentments.

□   Society holds misconceptions concerning stepparent-
hood. Who are stepparents? And how are they supposed to
act in the blended family unit?

Arthea, whose stepchildren live with her, resents the outside world's view of her role as a stepmother.

"I do everything for my stepchildren that a mother does
for her children. I wash their clothes. I cook their meals. I
pack their lunches. I pick up their dirty socks and underwear. And I wipe their runny noses. Yet because I'm not
their mother, but their stepmother, I have a lesser role
value than a 'real mother.' When I hear my stepchildren
say, 'She's not my real mother,' I want to ask them, 'What
does that make me? An unreal mother? A synthetic
mother?' I want to be recognized for being something in
their lives.

"My love is even regarded as less than 'real love.' Does
having to work at loving my stepchildren mean it isn't
love? That it's artificial? My husband automatically loves

his children, but I had to work ten times harder than he did for the love I have for them. He forgives them easily, while I have to labor in prayer to forgive them. I resent having all the responsibilities of motherhood, but being looked down upon by society as having less value and 'less love' because I'm a stepmother."

"I resent everybody's view of me," says Stan. "I think I'm an okay guy, but my family doesn't seem to have the same opinion. My wife thinks I'm a legalistic tough guy. My stepchildren think I'm unfair. The world thinks I'm not a real parent. To top it all off, my boss says I'm really not a full-time parent because my stepchildren visit their other household one day a week."

☐   Stepparents feel, in general, that a lack of control goes hand in hand with walking into a system that is already set up and operating on its own. To use corporate terms, instead of being one of the presidents or even a vice president in their blended family, stepparents feel more like consultants. The system can either accept or reject their ideas based on what the system wants. Or, as one stepparent put it, "It's like sitting and discussing something at a board meeting but then not being able to vote."

Jason agrees. "Who is the head of the household? Well, a stepfather is, when there aren't any problems. It's like being a fair-weather parent. When everybody's happy and getting along, I'm allowed to be head of the household. But let me voice my expectations or provide consequences when the children have acted up! Suddenly I no longer hold that position—my wife does. As far as she and the children are concerned, a stepfather cannot place demands on anyone in his family. I resent feeling so powerless. Now I know how eunuchs felt."

☐   Trying to enter a system with preexisting coalitions and alliances often makes stepparents feel like outsiders. Al's wife, Heather, who had been a single parent for eight years, had formed a strong alliance with her son. Al was in no way, shape or form allowed to be a member of this alliance, making him feel like an outsider.

"One Sunday afternoon as I sat in the living room trying to read the paper, I heard Heather and her son in the kitchen discussing where he had been the night before. The longer they talked, the more belligerent his attitude became. Thinking I should go to my wife's aid, I walked purposefully and sternly into the kitchen, wanting my stepson to realize I was in the room, and that he needed to control his tongue and change his attitude toward his mother. But instead of welcoming my support, my wife said, 'Go back into the other room and read your paper. I can take care of this.' I resent feeling as though it's the two of them and me, or, to be more accurate, the two of them against me."

☐   Like other family members, stepparents often enter a blended family with unrealistic expectations that eventually breed resentment.

"I just knew I was going to be a great stepmom. I was going to love Scott's three-year-old son, Stevie, just as I loved my children, and he would love me as his mom. One night before Scott and I were married, Stevie fell asleep in my arms on our way home from the park. At that moment I felt such love for Stevie because he was a part of Scott. I haven't held him like that since then.

"When Stevie came to visit on weekends right after Scott and I were married he cried because he missed his mom. When he was in one of those moods, he would not let me comfort him. He often got into things my children were trained to leave alone. Scott got upset with me whenever I corrected Stevie because he thought I was being too strict. My children began to resent Stevie and constantly complained, 'He gets away with everything.' Three realistic years later I feel more like a babysitter for my stepson than a stepmother. Sometimes I don't even think he likes me."

☐   Stepparents who do not have children from a previous marriage forfeit the dream of having a nuclear family for membership in a blended family.

"When I was a young girl, I used to dream about my future marriage and family," remembers Christi. "I pictured a handsome groom, my white satin wedding gown and, eventually, a child of my own.

"Then I met an older man named Stan who had custody of his two teenaged boys. Because he had been married before he refused to go through another wedding, so we were married at the courthouse.

When I said 'I do,' I walked out of my dream world right into a nightmare. One of Stan's sons used drugs and the other was uncontrollable. We spent the next three or four years getting them through one crisis after another.

"Now Stan blames me for some of his sons' difficulties, and they aren't real happy with me, either. The dream of having my own child is long gone: Stan has always said he's too old and, quite frankly, I'm burned out on parenting. I resent having given up a very real dream for Stan and his children, and then not being the least bit appreciated for doing it."

They may not admit it, but men also have dreams of what their wives will be like and how their family lives will be.

When Paul married Gretchen, a mother of two, he did not realize how much he would have to give up.

"I always pictured my wife and myself sleeping late on a Saturday morning. Then we would sit around the kitchen table sipping coffee and reading the paper together. You know—just relaxed and enjoying being together. Forget that! The moment Gretchen and I returned from our honeymoon we had to stop and pick up her kids. They clung to her for days. It was hard to find time to be alone with my wife, much less get romantic."

Loyalty Conflicts

"Having a magic wand would mean my wife would live by her own values instead of being torn between what I want and what her ex-mate or her children want."

Unlike biological parents, stepparents are not caught in the middle between two sides vying for loyalty. Instead, they are one of the competing sides.

☐   One of the leading complaints of stepparents in this area is, "You're more loyal to your children than you are to me." As a stepparent, I, too, have voiced that complaint. This disagreement between Adrienne and me may sound like a difference in parenting methods, but I experienced it as an issue of loyalty.

Adrienne had been complaining for days about having to nag the girls to make their beds and pick up their rooms before going to school. Because we both agreed on the behavior we wanted—clean bedrooms—we decided the best thing to do was to stop nagging and start applying consequences. Adrienne told Nichole and Jennifer that their beds had to be made and their rooms picked up before school every morning or they could not watch television or talk on the telephone that evening. They protested, but when they decided their mother was serious they complied grudgingly.

Our plan worked well at first, but after a few weeks the girls started coming up with excuses for not getting their chores done in the morning. Adrienne started to accept their excuses and began to let them do their rooms after school. Soon they were begging her to let them watch just one program while they were eating their after-school snacks. One program turned into two, then three. Before long the girls were watching TV and talking on the telephone—but their rooms were not done. Four nights out of five I would walk in from work, greet Nichole and Jennifer, go to my bedroom to change my clothes and find their rooms trashed and their beds unmade.

The first two or three times I accepted Adrienne's explanation that she forgot to follow through. After several weeks, however, I decided I could no longer accept her excuses. I felt Adrienne was making a choice between me and her children. I resented Adrienne's carrying out her children's wishes over mine, particularly when I thought hers and mine were originally the same.

☐   Stepparents often feel they are competing with the ex-mate for their spouse's loyalty.

James saw his wife's refusal to go to court for more child support as a loyalty issue.

"When I learned that my wife's ex-mate was supposed to pay twenty-five percent of his net income in child support, I was not happy with his paying only eleven or twelve percent," says James. "My wife, Joyce, knew as well as I did that we could use the extra money. Yet when I asked Joyce to take him back to court, she flatly refused. She was afraid her ex would try to get back at her through the children. For three years I asked her to go to court for more child support. No matter how hard I tried I couldn't help feeling she would rather make me work extra hours than put any financial strain on her ex's life. I resented her choosing her ex-mate's comfort over ours."

☐   Stepparents may also become involved in a conflict between the same-sex biological parent and their stepchildren. Even if the tension between a child's parent and same-sex stepparent is minimal, children are afraid that if they like their stepparent, they are being disloyal to their same-sex parent.

"My youngest stepdaughter, Annie, used to call me Mom until her older sister, Debbie, overheard her," says Sandra. "I heard Debbie tell her, 'I don't ever want to hear you call her that again. We already have a mom, and it's not Sandra.' Annie hasn't called me Mom since then. I resent my oldest stepdaughter destroying in one comment the relationship I had spent so long developing with Annie."

Blended Family Relationships

"If I had a magic wand I would wave in some new attitudes. Then my stepchildren would stop treating me like a nonperson without a heart or a brain, and my wife would stop worrying so much about bonding and start thinking about structure."

The Stepparent/Stepchild Relationship

☐   Stepparents' resentments about stepparent/stepchild relationships may center around the issue of bonding. Pete resents his wife's unrealistic expectations.

"My wife is constantly telling me, 'You don't love my children the same way I do.' I know I don't: They're *her* children, not mine. I resent hearing it all the time. She makes it sound like there's something wrong with me."

☐   When stepparents feel their mate is pushing bonding between them and their stepchildren they may see it as a form of manipulation and resent it.

Rex expressed discomfort and anger over his wife, Estelle's, attempts to force bonding between him and his stepson, John.

"I want bonding to occur naturally for my stepson and me, but Estelle keeps pushing it, buying me books on the subject and pointing out everything I'm 'not doing' to bond in this steprelationship.

"Estelle also tries to create artificial 'bonding' settings. She'll ask me to go to the store to pick up something she really doesn't need. When I'm on my way out the door, she'll inevitably say to John, 'Johnny, wouldn't you like to go with Dad in the truck?' John, who is really involved in a TV program, doesn't want to go. Estelle, set on getting the two of us to bond, makes him ride along with me. John pouts because it's my fault he missed his TV program, and I'm angry because I've been manipulated into going to the store for an unneeded item with a resentful stepson. Some bonding, huh, Estelle?"

☐   Biological parents may feel the relationship between their children and their mate is so fragile that any kind of disagreement between them will prevent future bonding. Consequently, biological parents may find themselves intervening in stepparent/stepchild disagreements, or trying to eliminate conflicts altogether. Chuck's experience shows that stepparents resent such interference.

"My wife, Ruth, never lets my stepdaughter and me come

to an agreement when we're arguing. She always intervenes. If asking us to forget the whole thing and go for an ice cream doesn't work, Ruth stays in the room and tries to start a discussion about something else, or sends her daughter to her room. I resent her for blocking bonding by interfering with our arguments. She doesn't realize bonding doesn't just occur when we go for ice cream; it can also take place when two people with differing opinions resolve their disagreement."

□   Stepparents may also come to resent overbonding in the parent/child relationship.

"I really don't know why Sally married me," says Randy. "Even when we were dating we didn't see a lot of each other; she was always doing something with her daughters. I thought it would change after we were married, but it hasn't. I had to make our bedroom off-limits for the girls, except by invitation only, because Sally and the girls would sit on our bed and talk for hours. It's our bedroom, not a girls' dorm.

"Their ability to communicate with their mom is good for the girls, but when my wife is having a problem I want her to talk to *me*. When she's had a good day at work, I want her to tell *me* about it. I resent her being so overbonded to the girls that there isn't any room left for me in her life."

□   Several stepparents have pegged their stepchildren's lack of respect as their number-one resentment.

"What frosts me? Being talked back to by my stepson. He won't talk back to his dad, but he'll talk back to me. Sometimes he's really blatant about it and at other times he just mumbles under his breath."

A stepfather voiced equal resentment over his stepchildren's lack of respect for their biological mother.

"They talk back to her and disregard her feelings. They are

constantly pushing to get their way with the ever-present threat that if they don't get what they want, they'll move out."

□   Like many other stepparents, Donald resented his step-children's lack of appreciation.

"I went to all of the school functions, ball games and concerts," Donald points out. "I'm the one who drove them to school every day of the week. I'm the one who felt responsible for their moral development. And I'm the one who had to be the hard guy when their grades weren't what they were supposed to be. I gave up personal time and things I wanted to do, to do things with them. It really hurts that after all of that sacrifice they now regard me as the enemy and talk about me to others as though I were an absolute jerk."

Beth's sixteen-year-old stepson, Ricky, went to live with his biological mother because her household had fewer rules and restrictions.

"I feel like a social worker who's given up a lot of private time to help an addict kick the habit—spending hours wrestling with him, fighting with him, talking to him, holding his head while he vomits and suffering with him—only to have him love his drug dealer more because he gives him what he wants: immediate gratification," says Beth. "I wasn't strict with Ricky because I was trying to fulfill some wicked stepmother role. I didn't do the things I did for him or spend time with him for fourteen years of his life because it was my duty. I did it because I love him. Now I resent being treated like some casual acquaintance because his mother gives him what he wants."

□   If a stepchild acts like or resembles the biological parent who is the same sex as the stepparent, and particularly if there is tension between households, the stepparent may resent the part of that stepchild's personality that is so much like the other biological parent.

"My stepchildren's mother is difficult to get along with," remarked Celeste, a mother/stepmother. "I don't like the way she runs down our Christian standards and our discipline style, and the way she gets her children to feel sorry for her and come to her defense. She's whiny, pouty and manipulative. When my stepchildren act the same way, I hit the roof."

The Couple Relationship

The couple relationship may be severely damaged if the stepparent feels his or her spouse is supporting an ex-mate or a biological child, in preference to him or her.

☐   Quinten felt his wife, Sheila, feared hurting her ex-mate's feelings more than hurting his. He felt she was choosing her ex-mate over him.

"Sheila's ex-mate called collect to talk to his children, and, boy, did I resent it. He doesn't even pay his court-ordered child support, and he expects me to pay for him to talk to his kids every week? The first time I got the phone bill, I saw red. I asked Sheila not to accept any more collect calls from her ex. I didn't care if the man was destitute, surely he could scrape up enough money to call his own kids.

"Sheila disagreed vehemently. She couldn't understand why I would want to cheat her children out of a phone call from their dad.

"In spite of Sheila's disagreement, the phone calls stopped, or so I thought. Then one afternoon I got home from work before Sheila did and picked up the mail. When I opened the phone bill I discovered her ex was calling just as often as before, except now he was calling to talk to his kids when I wasn't home. I not only resented her choosing her ex-mate's wishes over mine, but I resented her deception while doing it."

□   "When we were first married, I felt as though I was number one in Roger's life," says Deborah. "I was unaware, however, that Roger intended to get custody of his daughter, Gina, as soon as we were married. He began fighting his wife for more visitation time right after our wedding. Then he told me he wanted to go to court for permanent custody. I felt he had deceived me and I began to resent Gina's visits.

"One day Roger came home and informed me that he and his wife had agreed that Gina would live with us for six months out of the year. I was angry with Roger for not discussing it with me first, and told him we would have to talk about it before we made any definite plans. He gave me an ultimatum. 'If you won't let Gina stay, then you don't love me. If you don't love me, I guess it's over.' That scared me into withdrawing my stand.

"Ever since that day I have felt very insecure in our relationship. When Roger verbalized his ultimatum, I was demoted to number two in his life."

Discipline

"If I had a magic wand, I would wave it over my wife and make her consistent."

Stepparents often feel more resentment toward the whole issue of discipline than any other blended family issue. They resent their lack of control, the biological parent's failure to follow through on the rules, having a "bad guy" image, the children running to their biological parent and the biological parent's state of denial when it comes to the children's behavior.

□   A stepparent may wrestle with his or her mate's unwillingness to let the stepparent discipline the stepchildren
because "they aren't bonded."

During one of our seminars a stepfather commented, "My
wife wants me to bond with her children, but she doesn't
want me to provide any discipline whatsoever." To which a
stepmother quickly added, "Even when I'm just trying to
follow through with my husband's rules, I have to fight not
only his kids, but him." Another stepparent agreed. "My
wife is so preoccupied with bonding, she ignores her children's need for structure and discipline."

□   Once a biological parent and stepparent sit down together and decide on the household rules, the stepparent may
become angry over his or her mate's refusal to follow through
on the agreed-upon rules.

"Whenever my wife, Anita, and I work out a specific rule
for the children, I know she will disregard or bend the rule
we have agreed upon," says Jerry. "When we bought some
new furniture for our living room, Anita and I agreed there
would be no eating in there. For me it is a black-and-white
issue: You are either eating in the living room, or you are not
eating in the living room. Anita, on the other hand, sees
everything as gray. When her children come home after
school and want a snack, it just happens to be the same time
their favorite TV program is on. If your favorite TV program is on and you're hungry, in Anita's mind, you're not
really eating in the living room.

"When Anita comes home from work and finds cookie
crumbs on the couch, she doesn't try to find out who was
eating there. If her children were sneaky enough to eat in the
living room without being seen, they really have not broken
the rule. I don't buy that. I have found a banana peel, a

Twinkie and potato chips smashed under the cushions on the couch. I knew Anita would ignore this rule as soon as she had to apply a consequence for her children's misbehavior. I follow through on the rules we have agreed on. Why can't she?"

☐   When biological parents do not follow through on the rules but stepparents do, the stepparents acquire a bad image. Because Anita would not follow through with the "no eating in the living room" rule or apply consequences when she found cookie crumbs on the couch, Jerry appeared mean in the children's eyes, and strict in his wife's eyes, when he enforced the rule.

☐   When children, step or biological, detect a discrepancy between parents concerning rules and follow-through, they will often work it to their advantage. If they discover their biological parent can find exceptions to the rule and their stepparent is the 'enforcer,' they will run to their biological parent every time, thus turning discipline into a loyalty issue.

This happened in Teresa's blended family.

"My husband, Jesse, and I both work. Because I get home from work before Jesse, I'm the one who finds his children's coats, books, lunchboxes, shoes and snack trails all over the house. When I tell them to clean up the mess they have made, they disappear. Later I see them greeting Jesse in the driveway, telling him, 'You'd better watch out, Dad, Teresa's on the warpath again.' By the time he walks in the door, I'm furious. When I tell him about the mess his children made and their disappearing act, he looks at his kids and says, 'You're right, she *is* on the warpath.' Jesse reacts to the whole situation by making excuses for his children and acting like there is something wrong with me. I resent the way my stepchildren run to their dad every time I ask them to do something. And I resent Jesse's letting them get away with it."

Family Bonding

"If I had a magic wand, taking a week's family vacation with 'hers,' 'mine' and 'ours' would be a time of fun and family bonding, instead of like going to the great abyss and back."

Family milestones such as birthdays, graduations, weddings, holidays and, yes, even vacations enhance bonding in the nuclear family. In the blended family, however, such milestones may intensify feelings of loss, sorrow and conflicting loyalties.

☐   Someone is always left behind when a blended family goes on a family trip, due to the shifting of family composition, scheduling and ties to the other household. Putting together day and night for a week children who see each other only one day a week or every other weekend can lead to a crazy, loud and tense vacation.

Last year Phillip wanted to take a family vacation. This year he wants to take a fishing trip—by himself.

"My wife, Lynn, and I wanted to take a family vacation to help cement our family bonds. We took her two girls, who live with us, and my three boys, who live with their mother, to Disney World. The trip was a disaster from start to finish.

"The boys' mother, who was angry because I was taking them where I had never taken her, didn't pack enough clothes for them. My stepdaughters had already been to Disney World with their father. Every time I turned around I heard how great he was and how much fun they had had with him on that vacation. My boys worried constantly about their mother and wanted to call her every day. My youngest son sobbed uncontrollably two or three times, wanting to go home and see Mommy.

"My boys and Lynn's girls competed continually for my wife's and my attention. My boys were afraid I was going to show more affection to, buy more Cokes for and ride on more rides with my stepdaughters than them. My stepdaughters didn't think it was fair that we bought new clothes for my boys, even though they didn't have anything to wear.

"By the time we headed home, my wife and I were not speaking, my stepdaughters and sons were close to killing each other and the loyalty dividing line between her family and my family was so thick you could almost cut it with a knife."

☐   Sometimes stepchildren hurt a stepparent by blocking family bonding.

"When Sam's two boys, Joey and Thad, come to stay with us, I always try to think of fun things to do together as a family," explains June. "They never like my ideas, especially if I'm part of the plan. The last time they were here, I suggested to Sam that we take the boys for ice cream. Sam, thinking it was a good idea, went to call the boys.

"The boys thought it was a great idea, too. They raced each other to the car, scuffling over who was going to sit in the front seat with their dad. When they saw me walk out of the house, Joey turned to his dad and said, 'Is she going? Then I don't want to go.'

"We all went, with an unhappy Joey in the back seat. By the time we got where we were going, I didn't feel much like working on bonding. All of my energy was now focused on trying not to be angry. It's always the same thing. Even when we try to do little things as a family to bond, Joey blocks it."

The Other Household

"If I had a magic wand, I would make my husband's ex-mate disappear. Then her presence and opinions would no longer be felt in our household."

The resentments stepparents feel toward the other household revolve around their mate's ex-spouse, visitation, holidays and the loyalty conflict between households.

Mate's Ex-Spouse

☐   "My wife's ex, George, lives across town, but he carries a lot of weight in this household," complains Terry. "It doesn't matter what I say in our home, if George says something different, in my stepchildren's eyes he's always right and I'm always wrong. My wife even worries about what George says, what he thinks, what he does and what he has. Frankly, I've felt for quite some time that he might as well live here."

☐   Terry also resents feeling that he and George are rivals competing between households.

"Besides always being right, George also manages to do everything first. If I tell my stepchildren we're going to do or get anything, their father somehow manages to beat us to it.

"My wife and I decided to buy a camcorder to record our children at ball games, school events and just for fun at home. For us, it was a major expense. We began setting money aside, anticipating reaching our goal in nine months. As soon as George heard about our family project, he went right out and bought a camcorder. Not only did my stepchildren enjoy the camcorder in their other household first, but they bring home videos they have recorded over there to play on our VCR. I hate the way he constantly pushes me to compete with him."

☐   Ellen was less concerned about the unseen presence of her husband's ex-wife, Eva, than she was about Eva's negative influence on her stepchildren's lives.

"For years I could almost handle the way Eva was undermining all of the Christian training we were giving my stepchildren. She purposely let them know that she approved of things we didn't. Eva allowed them to watch pay TV in her home and took them to movies we considered unacceptable. But I always thought that as long as the kids lived in our home and were going to church with their father and me, we could offset her negative influence.

"Last month Eva was awarded custody. Suddenly, and much to my stepchildren's delight, they have been thrown into a world of adult privileges and adult responsibilities. At the ages of fourteen and fifteen, they are just not ready. I resent Eva for appealing to their immaturity with her own lack of morality."

Visitation

☐   For some stepparents, visitation is more of a trauma than a treat. One stepmother compares her stepchildren's visits to a zoo—minus the fun, but with plenty of little animals.

Another stepmother was angry at her husband's lack of effort and empathy when his children visited.

"I resent my husband's unwillingness to help out with household chores when his children are staying with us. I have to plan, cook and clean up after meals, pick up continually and do more laundry. Why can't he help out when they're here? After all, they're his kids."

☐   When the visitation period is completely devoted to a mate's biological children, the stepparent may feel excluded and resentful.

"I understand my husband, Jonathan's, need to spend time with his daughter," says Andrea, "but the way the two of them giggle and whisper makes me feel like we are all in high school and I'm on the outside watching the 'in group' have a good time. They talk about people I don't know, laugh about old family jokes and pick things to do that aren't fun for me. It's not until she leaves that I become Jonathan's wife again."

☐   Rick, on the other hand, resents the way his wife, Lucy, shows favoritism to her children over his children, who live with them.

"Lucy always twists everything to accommodate her two boys. The rule in our household at mealtime is, you can take as much food as you want, but you eat as much as you take. If you don't finish what's on your plate, there is no dessert. If my children ask for dessert without cleaning their plates, Lucy consistently tells them no. When her boys come to stay, they pile enough food on their plates for two meals and don't even make a dent in it. When they ask for dessert, they always get it.

"On the weekends her boys come to visit, Lucy makes sure my children are in bed by their regular bedtime, while hers stay up later. She allows her children to talk back to her. If my children even 'take a tone,' she jumps all over them."

☐   Doug wants his stepchildren to enjoy the time they spend in their other household. But he *does* resent getting the cold shoulder when they return.

"I generally get along pretty well with my stepchildren. When they return from their other household, however, they treat me like a total stranger. I resent having to deal with this change in attitude toward me once every week. If they didn't have to go to another household, my relationship with my stepchildren wouldn't be in a constant state of flux."

□   Stepparents also resent the upheavals that result when stepchildren must live by two sets of rules in two separate households.

"When my stepkids go to their other household, they can watch whatever they want on TV," says Max. "When they come home, they try to 'sneak-watch' the same type of programs, even though they know we don't approve. Because their dad thinks these programs are okay, their mother and stepfather look 'Victorian' by comparison.

"Although their father is much more lenient than we are in our household, when he does discipline it carries more weight with the children than when we correct them. When I try to discipline my stepchildren they look at me like, 'Who are you and what right do you have to be saying this to us?' "

Holidays

Holidays, which should be filled with fun and family time, are often the most difficult days and seasons of the year.

□   Eric made these comments about Christmas at his household.

"Our Christmas is never important. Whatever we have to do, we'd better do it quick. It has to be rushed because the children have to get to their dad's and his relatives on time. Our Christmas is just something my stepchildren endure until they can get to the real celebration at their father's house."

□   Katrina discovered that the blending of families also necessitated the blending of Christmas traditions. When that didn't happen, she felt resentful.

"It was a tradition for my children and me to hang homemade ornaments on our Christmas tree, while Fred and his children collected expensive ornaments. When it came time to trim the tree, Fred put the tree up, I put the lights on and we went upstairs to the kitchen to have some hot cocoa while the children put on the garland and ornaments. It wasn't long before my daughter, Jeanie, came running upstairs crying. My stepchildren had informed my children that our ornaments weren't good enough for their tree. When we went downstairs the tree looked beautiful, but not one of our homemade ornaments was hanging on it. I resented my stepchildren's audacity."

Loyalty Conflicts Between Households

Stepparents often feel the repercussions of loyalty conflicts between households.

☐   "It's easy to tell when my stepchildren have been listening to their father and stepmother put down our home," one stepfather confided. "My wife and I are very careful what we say concerning the other household, and I resent having the other household slam us, forcing our children into a loyalty conflict."

☐   Trudy, a stepmother of two, discovered that loyalty problems she thought were resolved cropped up again unexpectedly.

"I really thought that once we had the bonds and love established, they were established. I resent seeing that after five or six good years, when my stepchildren hit adolescence, the other household looks more attractive than ours to them because it has fewer restrictions."

As a stepparent reading "your" chapter, you may have been checking box after box, identifying your resentments. You may have said to yourself, "Yes, that's exactly how I feel," or, "I didn't know anyone else felt that way." If you are a biological parent *and* a stepparent, you undoubtedly have boxes checked in both chapters.

As you read on and learn what your children and your stepchildren are feeling, you will probably realize that most of the problems and difficulties you face in your blended family are inherent in the system, not the people.

And systems can be changed. Before we explore that area, however, let's see how children in blended families feel.

— 5 —

Children's Resentments

"When Dad married Maggie, everything changed," says seventeen-year-old Kenny. "I'm living in a different house in a different state and going to a bigger high school. My stepbrother, Jeff, who's only seven months older than me, lives with us. He's one of those smart, do-everything well, ladykiller-type jocks all of us guys secretly wish we could be. I'm not smart. I'm just average. And I think I've only had four dates in my whole life.

"About two months after school started, Jeff told Maggie he wanted to live with his dad in Michigan, so he moved out. It was great. I was an only child again. Three months later he was back. Now Dad and Maggie are talking about having Cindy, my sixteen-year-old stepsister, come to live with us, too. That's all I need!

"I only see my mom, who lives in California, two weeks in the summer. I hate having her so far away; I worry about her a lot. Whenever I start to have a good time, it's like a little voice goes off inside my head saying, *How can you be happy when your mom's so miserable?* Or when I start thinking, *Hey,*

Maggie's really not so bad, that little voice pops into my mind again and says, *You can't like Maggie, she's not your real mom."*

Children's experiences in a blended family are as unique as those of adult family members. Children's resentments surround the same basic themes as their parents' and stepparents', but focus on different issues. What would children living in blended families change if they had a magic wand?

The System

"If I had a magic wand, my mom and dad would be back together."

It is common for children living in blended families to drag their feet, literally and symbolically, over the changes resulting from divorce and remarriage: "I didn't choose this system, the divorce, the remarriage, the move to a new home or school. I didn't choose this stepparent, these stepbrothers and stepsisters, or to live in two households."

□   "I didn't choose the divorce." With that one statement children in blended families describe their loss and the lack of control they have over their lives.

"I was outside playing at my friend's house when Mom called me in," says Rachel. "She looked so serious. When I walked into the living room, there was Dad sitting on the couch. I didn't know what was going on, but all of a sudden I felt like crying. Dad motioned for me to sit down next to him. I don't remember what he said or how he said it. All I knew was my daddy was leaving me; he was going to live somewhere else and he wasn't taking me with him.

"I hated the unfairness of it all. In the morning I was playing outside just like any other day. In the afternoon I was bawling my eyes out because my daddy was gone. I didn't want my mom and dad to get a divorce. I wanted everything to stay the way it was."

When divorced or widowed adults remarry, they and their children are on different emotional wavelengths. The adults look at the occasion as a new beginning; the children view it through the eyes of loss.

In divorce children lose a daily parent/child relationship with at least one parent. When remarriage occurs, they ask, "Will I still see my dad or mom who is being replaced by this new stepparent?" Watching a parent walk down the aisle on the arm of someone other than Mom or Dad destroys their hopes of a parental reunion. For most children at that moment, bringing a stepparent into the family is not a gain, but a confirmation of the permanency of their loss.

As children become part of a new blended family system, they silently ask themselves, *Where do I fit in?* This new beginning means they will have to share their parent with another adult and possibly with new stepbrothers and stepsisters.

☐   For Claudia remarriage meant a change in roles.

"I didn't want Mom to get remarried: I liked things just the way they were. Before Mom married Jay, we used to talk a lot and do things together. Mom doesn't talk to me about her problems anymore—she tells Jay. I used to be number one in her life, but I feel like the love she had for me has been taken away and given to him. There's love connecting all around me, but it's not *for* me. Mom and I used to be like best friends, but now I'm just a dumb kid again."

☐   Other children experience an instant change in birth order when their parents remarry. This shift can vary from household to household and from day to day.

"Before Dad married Gretchen, I was the youngest kid in our family," explains Anna. "I got extra attention and I don't think I got into as much trouble for doing the same things everybody else did. If something had to be done, my parents almost always asked my oldest brother, Tim. Now all of a sudden I have two younger stepbrothers, and I'm hearing, 'Anna, would you watch your little brothers while we're gone?' and, 'Anna, why did you let him do that? You're old enough to know better.' I don't like having to take care of my stepbrothers, and I don't like being a middle child.''

☐   A parent's remarriage often means children have to move into a new house in a new neighborhood, or maybe even a new state. After Danny's mother remarried he went from being a big fish in a little pond to being a little fish in the ocean.

"When Mom married Wes, we moved from a small town to a mega-metropolis. The high school I go to now is four times the size of the high school I went to back home. Back home I was the star of the football team and the baseball team, and I was a good basketball player. When I walked down the hall everyone knew me, and dates were no problem.

"When I walked down the hall on my first day at school here I didn't know anyone and no one knew me. I'm not popular. I'm not the superstar. I'm so ticked at Mom for dragging me here and taking me away from my friends.''

☐   Children living in blended families are often quick to point out they didn't choose their stepparent, and they "sure wouldn't have picked this person who is so different from Mom or Dad.''

Karla resented being stuck with a domineering, take-charge stepfather.

"I don't know if my stepfather, Neil, expected me to be just like my two stepsisters or if he had some mental picture of how a kid should act. Anyway, I don't fit his picture. When things go wrong, or if he thinks I'm not doing something the right way, he jumps on me about it. I just keep telling Mom, 'I'm doing the same things the same way I've always done them. It's not my fault. *You* wanted him here. *I* didn't.' "

☐   The very presence of stepbrothers and stepsisters, not to mention their personality types, also generates resentment. Victor was an only child whose quiet life was invaded by three noisy, wild stepsiblings.

"My three stepbrothers drive me right up the wall. Whenever they come over to spend the weekend they go into my bedroom and tear up my stuff. I'm supposed to pretend it really doesn't matter. They act like pigs at the table, and they always eat all the good stuff before I have a chance to get any. They never walk anywhere: They always run or karate-chop their way around or jump on my bed. Because I'm older, Dad and Grace have me watch my stepbrothers while they run errands. I didn't ask to have stepbrothers. And if I had I sure wouldn't have picked the bratty ones I've got."

☐   Children in blended families have to adjust to the loss of continuity built into the two-household system with its differences in lifestyles, rules and displays of affection. Confusion and bewilderment often result.

"I live with Mom and Lyle, and have a stepbrother, David, and a stepsister, Wendy, who come over every weekend," says Megan. "When it comes to my stepdad, I don't know when I'm doing something right or wrong, especially when David and Wendy come over. They never get in trouble for the same things I get in trouble for.

"My dad never remarried. When I stay with him I just sit around all day and watch TV until he gets home. Sometimes

I cook us supper, but Dad doesn't have much of the kind of food you cook. We just mostly eat snack food. Dad's had a lot of different girlfriends, which is okay with me. They always treat me nice to stay on Dad's good side.

"Going back and forth between Mom's and Dad's can get real confusing. I don't like having two households that are so different."

☐   Children, like adults, often enter the blended family system with unrealistic expectations. Carey, an only child, was excited about having a sister when her mother remarried.

"I wasn't too hot on the idea of Curt being my stepfather, but I really liked the idea of having a sister. I wanted to be best buddies with his daughter, Mary Jo. But it didn't work out that way. Mary Jo never wanted to do anything with me, and when she and Curt went somewhere she never wanted me to come along. Sometimes Mom had to fight with them so they would take me; then Mary Jo really didn't like me. I wanted to be best friends in the worst way, but Mary Jo just wouldn't cooperate."

Susie thought her mom's marriage to Lloyd would bring her the father she longed for.

"My real dad left us when I was just a baby, and I've never met him. I really wanted a dad to love me and take care of Mom and me, but things haven't worked out the way I expected. My stepdad doesn't show me any kind of emotion except when he's mad at me. In fact, we can go for a whole month without talking to each other. It really hurts that he hasn't tried, even a little, to get to know me. Some days I just ache so much inside that I want to scream at him, 'Talk to me! I'm not a bad person.' At other times I want to beg him to be my dad."

Loyalty Conflicts

"If I had a magic wand, everyone would quit thinking that everything I do is because I have chosen sides with someone else."

It is not unusual for children in blended families to be caught in more than one loyalty conflict at a time, torn between their biological parents, their parent and stepparent, their parent and same-sex stepparent, and their parent and stepsiblings and half-siblings.

☐   Children often find themselves caught between their biological parents, especially if unresolved conflicts remain from the divorce. Denny resented his mother's and father's overinterpretation of everything he did.

"Every time I do something with Dad, Mom thinks I've chosen to be on his side. If I decide to do something with Mom, Dad thinks I've chosen to be on her side. If Mom and Dad would just take care of the problems they have with each other my life would be a whole lot easier. When are my parents going to see how much I hate it when they put me in the middle? They're the adults. Why can't they understand that I can love them both?"

☐   In the loyalty conflict between the biological parent and the stepparent, the children are not in the middle choosing between two sides. They are competing with their stepparent for their parent's time, attention or affection.

"I get so mad at Mom because she won't stick up for me," says Lisa. "When my stepfather, Leonard, starts in on me about chewing with my mouth open or having my elbows on the table, Mom doesn't say a word. When Leonard goes on and on about something that I know she thinks is acceptable, I keep looking to Mom for support, but there isn't any. The way I see it, Mom loves Leonard more than me."

☐   Children can also feel they are competing with step-siblings or half-siblings for their parent's attention. Gwen was afraid her stepsister, Danielle, would take her place in her dad's life.

"I really hate having Danielle live with my dad. She gets to do things with him every day and I just do things with him on Saturdays. What if he starts loving her more than me?"

☐   Children caught in a loyalty conflict between their biological parent and their same-sex stepparent often feel (as we have seen) that they are being disloyal to their parent just by liking their stepparent.

"My stepdad likes to do things that I like to do, like camping and fishing," explains Wesley. "My dad doesn't like any of that stuff. But I still love my dad because he's my dad. I decided last weekend not to visit my dad so I could go fishing with my stepdad, but I felt so guilty the whole time, neither of us had a very good time."

Blended Family Relationships

"If I had a magic wand, my stepdad would stop trying to run my life, my mother would stick up for me and my stepbrothers would stay out of my room."

The Stepchild/Stepparent Relationship

☐   Stepchildren's resentments, when it comes to the stepchild/stepparent relationship, may center around the issue of authority. "I don't have to listen to you; you're not my father [mother]," stepparents often hear. One stepchild was quick to share his point of view concerning his stepfather's authority.

"My mother, my stepfather and I have one basic disagreement: They both think my stepfather has the right to tell me what to do. But he's not anything to me. He's just my mother's husband."

☐   While some stepchildren act as if they could care less about what their stepparent thinks, other stepchildren are seeking their stepparent's approval.

"I don't measure up to my stepfather's standards," says Lana. "No matter what I do I'm not as good as his children. That really hurts. If Jack, my stepfather, trips over a shoe, it's my fault. One day I just decided I don't care if Jack doesn't like me. I'll just do my own thing. He's never going to approve of anything I do anyway."

☐   A stepparent's negative attitude toward the same-sex biological parent often leads to anger and resentment on the part of the stepchild.

"I hate it when my stepdad says bad things about my dad," Jason told us. "I know he isn't perfect, but he's my dad. Whenever my stepdad starts cutting my dad down, especially when he's talking to my mother, I don't even want to live in the same house with him."

The Child/Parent Relationship

☐   Some children don't want to take responsibility for anything. Other children, like Aaron, feel responsible for everything, including their parents' divorce.

"I felt bad about leaving Dad behind when I went to live with my mom and stepdad. Dad would call and ask me when I was coming back. After staying with Mom for a while, I decided to move back with Dad, who had also remarried. I had only been back a week when I knew I had made a mistake.

"My stepmother, Audrey, and I did not get along at all. I told Dad I just couldn't take it any longer and moved back in with Mom. I was only back with Mom for two months when Dad called and said, 'I've gotten rid of your stepmom. You can come home now.' I didn't tell him to do that. Sometimes I feel responsible for Mom and Dad's divorce, even though I know it really wasn't my fault. And now I resent my dad for making me feel responsible that his second marriage didn't work out."

☐   Kevin doesn't feel responsible for his parents' divorce, but he does feel responsible for the parent he feels was left behind.

"Dad married Karen and I live with them. I see Mom once a year and worry about her all the rest of the time. I know she's doing stuff she shouldn't be doing, a lot of partying and that sort of thing. She sold insurance for a while but that didn't work out. Then she tried real estate, and had to file bankruptcy. Dad's had to pay for my plane tickets the last two years and I don't think he's going to do it again this year. Mom needs someone to take care of her. I think about moving in with her, but I'd probably end up being the parent. I hate being the one who has to worry about her all of the time."

☐   When one parent is not divorced emotionally from the other parent and conflict results, it is not unusual for the children to be caught in the crossfire.

"My dad says some pretty nasty things about Mom. He and my stepmother are always running her down. I usually end up defending Mom, but then I can't help but wonder why she left us. When Dad says such crummy things about Mom, it's like he's shooting arrows at her, but they go right through my heart."

☐   Many children fear losing their noncustodial parent's love.

"I feel more responsible for my relationship with my dad, whom I don't live with, than for my relationship with my mom, whom I do live with," comments Janice. "I guess it's because I'm afraid my dad will stop loving me. He's already physically gone. What's to stop him from taking a hike emotionally? I'm the one who has to call him or ask him to come and pick me up to do something. I get tired of feeling responsible for keeping the relationship with my father going."

The Child/Stepsibling and Half-Sibling Relationship

☐   The battle between stepsiblings over what they consider to be unfair treatment can be fierce. Not only do stepsiblings often compete for the adults' attention in a blended family, they also contend with the issue of fairness.

Madalyn felt her stepmother was being unfair when it came to a particular household chore.

"I have a stepsister who is a year older than I am. My stepmother folds her underwear and puts it neatly in her drawer. She puts mine in a laundry basket on my bed. That may not seem like a big deal, but it says a lot to me: It says I'm just not important to my stepmother. When I talked to my dad about it and he talked to my stepmom, she told him it was just a lot of nonsense."

☐   Lance's resentment toward his half-sister was not over unfair treatment, but over the unfairness of the system.

"I'm so jealous of my half-sister. She has her mom and dad here, while my mom lives here with my stepdad and my dad lives in another house with my stepmom. Besides that, she's the youngest; she gets babied and she never gets in trouble."

Discipline

"If I had a magic wand, my mom would be my only boss in this house and my dad would be my only boss in his house. And neither one of them would be very bossy."

Complaints concerning discipline voiced by children living in blended families often revolve around the stepparent and stepsiblings.

☐   Children in blended families have their own ideas about who has the right to discipline and who doesn't.

One teenage stepson said, "I resent my stepdad coming in as the big disciplinarian when he won't even take the time to talk to me."

Another stepchild added:

"My stepdad came right in and took charge. When I ask Mom if I can do something, she never answers until she runs and asks my stepdad what he thinks. Then what he says goes, even if Mom doesn't really agree. There are times when I can argue with Mom and she'll give in. If my stepdad's around, forget it. He's Mister Rigid. I resent my mother for this. I'm her kid, not his."

☐   When the stepparent is also a biological parent, the stepchildren may feel there is unequal treatment between them and their stepsiblings. Jordan, a seventeen-year-old, did not appreciate what he considered to be his stepfather's eagerness to correct him and his unwillingness to discipline his own children.

"My stepdad, Bill, always comes down hard on me in front of everybody, but he never corrects my stepbrother, Bo. Bo and I had both started smoking. They caught me once or twice. So every time they smelled cigarette smoke, they automatically thought it was mine. I didn't tell on Bo, because, hey, I was smoking, too. One time when Mom found a pack of cigarettes and asked me about them, I just said, 'They're not my brand.'

"One night when Bill and Mom had company, Bill had smelled cigarette smoke in the car earlier and assumed it was my fault. He jumped all over me in front of the company. I hadn't even used the car. Bo had. Mom finally said, 'Bo, isn't there something you want to tell your dad?' Even though Bo confessed, my stepdad didn't say a word to him. He didn't say anything to me, either. He never said he was sorry or that he had been wrong. And as far as I know Bo never did get in trouble for smoking in the car. Every time I break the rules it's a felony. If Bo does, it's a misdemeanor.''

Family Bonding

"If I had a magic wand, I'd feel as though I were part of a real family."

☐   Some children, eager to regain the security and normalcy of family living, work willingly on family bonding. Others, however, find a sense of family belonging hard to come by.

"The only time my stepdad wants to do anything with Mom and me is when it's something he wants to do or when his kids are here. When I ask him if we can go someplace or do something he always says, 'Why don't you and your mom go, and we'll do something later when Tommy and Allen are here?' When my stepbrothers are here we do what they want to do. Then he's not doing anything fun with me, he's doing what they want to do with them.''

☐   Their lack of control over the divorce and remarriage leaves some children angry and uncooperative. Others, strug-

gling with divided loyalties and the fear that they may lose
this family, too, sometimes demonstrate a lack of commitment to their blended family unit. Still other children rebel
against bonding with a family that has made reconciliation
between their parents even more remote.

Family bonding is more difficult when the children are
adolescents at the time of their parents' remarriage. At the
same time that their parents want their adolescent children to
bond with this new family, the children are working on be-
coming independent.

"Ever since my mother married Barney, she keeps planning all of these dumb things to do as a family," complains
Eddie. "I don't want to be part of her new family. I've got
my friends and things I want to do. This new family wasn't
my idea and I resent having to change my plans in order to go
along with it."

Living in Two Households

*"If I had a magic wand there would be only one house to live in:
It would be mine, and my parents would move in and out."*

Some children cannot understand the concept of permeable
and impermeable boundaries between households. The children, whose household boundaries are permeable, often want
their parents to celebrate birthdays, graduations and holidays
together as one big happy family. They either fail to realize
the adults' need for clear-cut psychological boundaries and
well-defined physical boundaries between households, or
they are still holding onto the fantasy of a parental reunion.
The children may resent their parents' unwillingness to "get
along" when the parents are simply respecting each other's
family boundaries.

Children may also resent living in two households because it complicates their lives. Different rules, different expectations and confusion over whether something happened "here" or "there" often prevent a settled routine.

☐ Lucy, now in her early twenties, shared how frustrated and resentful she felt when she was younger over the different rules and expectations in her two households.

"There were always different rules in my two families. I recognize now that it is because my mom and dad have very different personalities, which I didn't understand when I was growing up. Before I said or did anything I had to stop and ask myself, 'Whose house am I in?' Mom's house emphasized moral behavior and treating people kindly, while Dad's house stressed working hard and getting good grades. I felt that I had to live up to the standards at Mom's house, carry them with me to Dad's house, live up to the standards at Dad's house, and bring them all back to Mom's house. Having so many different rules and standards to live up to made me crazy. I had to be a super-kid."

Visitation

The constant transition between households further complicates the lives of children living in blended families. Children need *time, space, "stuff"* and *respect* in order to travel successfully between households.

☐ When they first enter the other household children need time to adjust, to get reacquainted, to find out what took place while they were gone and what the rest of the family is talking about. Jana resented her parents for not giving her a little adjustment time when she moved back and forth between households.

"I sometimes feel like a stranger when I go to my 'other'

household, no matter which one it is. When I walk in, everyone's talking about things that happened while I was gone. I feel left out. Sometimes I wish they would all stop talking and tell me what happened so I can feel like part of the family, too."

When children reenter a household they may need some "alone time" to work through the feelings of having to leave their other parent and their other household.

"When I go to see my dad I feel weird," said Peter, "like we really don't know each other. After awhile he's my dad again. But then it's time for me to go back home, and I hate saying goodbye. When I get home, my mom's standing at the door waiting for me. She calls my stepdad in and they starting fussing over me. I hate that. I don't know how to explain it, but I wish they would just leave me alone for a while."

☐   Space and "stuff" are just as important to children as they are to adults.

"I feel like a visitor when I stay at my dad's house," Joel remarks. "I sleep in the family room on a sleeping bag I bring with me. Because it's the family room, I have to wait until everybody's ready to go to bed before *I* can. I really hate not having a special place to be by myself if I want to, or to put some of my things and leave them there."

☐   Space and "stuff" are equally important for the custodial child, as in Marie's case.

"When my stepsister comes to visit, she's always trying on my clothes and asking to borrow something. I wouldn't mind so much if she would only take the things I tell her she can wear. She gets into my stuff without telling me and when I see it again, *if* I see it again, it's all wadded up and dirty. I resent her invading my room."

Holidays

As we saw from the parents' perspective, holidays in two households are not only hectic for everyone, but they can be sources of resentment for everyone. Before the remarriage, both the husband's and the wife's nuclear family had particular holiday traditions. When these differ, or when there is conflict between traditions and scheduling, feelings get hurt and resentments are born. Children are no exception.

□   Barbara had her own ideas about how Christmas should be celebrated.

"Mom and I always put our Christmas tree up the day after Thanksgiving. My stepdad and his kids want to put it up two weeks before Christmas because his kids won't be here at Thanksgiving. And everyone knows you open your presents on Christmas morning, not on Christmas Eve. This Christmas we're not putting our tree up until my stepdad decides we can, and we're opening presents when his kids come over Christmas Eve. It makes me mad that we have to do everything their way."

□   Traditions and schedules are not the children's only source of resentment during the holidays. Children feel their losses more acutely then, too.

"On Christmas Eve when I'm at my dad's, I feel guilty if I have a good time because Mom's not there," said Ricky, a young teen. "Then when I go to Mom's house on Christmas Day I feel bad because Dad's not there. Christmas isn't fun anymore. It's great getting lots of presents, but I'd give them all up just to have my family together during the holidays. I hate feeling guilty, sad and rushing everywhere during the Christmas holidays."

☐   As we mentioned in chapters 3 and 4, resentment over gift-giving is not unusual in blended families. Children in blended families tend to view material gifts as a way of measuring how much they are loved. Following that premise they may reason, "If my stepsiblings or half-siblings get more gifts, my stepparent (or parent) must love them more than me." Children's jealousy over the amount of presents brought back by their stepsiblings into the custodial home from the noncustodial household leads to resentments.

Loyalty Conflicts Between Households

Children often have divided loyalties concerning their households, with the severity depending a great deal on the relationship between their biological parents. In Brian's case, the relationship between households was harsh indeed.

"My other brother, Arnold, and I lived with our Mom. Mom wanted Arnold, who's hyperactive and a real pain in the neck, to live with Dad. Dad told Mom we could either live with him or with Mom, but he wasn't going to split us up. Mom finally agreed to let us both live with Dad. When I visited Mom out of state, Arnold seldom went with me. One night I heard Dad telling a friend that Mom always managed to work out my visits to her at times when Arnold couldn't go.

"The last time I visited Mom, she told me I was going to live with her and she wasn't going to send me on the plane back home to Dad. I may be only ten, but I'm smart enough to put two and two together: Mom just wanted to get rid of Arnold.

"Being around Arnold is really a hassle, but I feel bad Mom doesn't want him. I want to go back home with Dad and Arnold, but I'm all Mom's got. And besides, I don't think she would buy me a plane ticket. I know Arnold and I are just kids, but I hate not having any say about whose house I live in or whether or not I can see my own brother and my dad."

☐ Her mother's inability to separate emotionally from her father put Kathleen in a loyalty bind.

"I hate being in the middle. When I return home from staying with my dad, my mom asks me, 'How was the weekend? What did you do?' I know if I answer she'll start asking about my dad and stepmom. 'How are they getting along? Has your stepmother lost any weight yet? Did your dad get his promotion? Have they bought anything new?' My mom makes me so angry when she does that. She's asking me to betray Dad."

So Where's the Magic Wand?

The goal of these last three chapters has been to enable each blended family member to identify and (potentially) express how he or she feels. Accurately defining resentments will enhance the way you deal with those feelings within yourself and within your blended family.

When blending is not taking place, it is often because these resentments have taken root. You may have become frustrated with the numerous obstacles to overcome; disappointment in your mate, the children and your marriage; and disappointment in yourself. You may feel hopeless concerning your inability to create a family out of all of this chaos. This ambiguous suprasystem called a blended family looks overwhelming. Many blended family members throw their hands up in the air saying, "I give up. I quit. It's just too hard."

Don't give up. Don't throw your hands up in despair. Adrienne and I have met well-functioning, happy blended families that have not only identified their problems, but have set out to resolve their difficulties and conflicts.

So where's the magic wand? As you may have guessed, none exists. The circumstances you are experiencing as a member in a blended family, and the feelings that go along with them, cannot be changed that easily. But they can be changed. We have a big God. When we follow His program He adds the strength, the grace and the understanding necessary to make our blended family healthy and functional.

— 6 —

First Steps

Imagine that you, your mate, your children and your stepchildren are sitting in my office. We have decided in advance to make this a Saturday marathon counseling session, and we have spent the last three hours (or three chapters) with everyone taking turns voicing resentments and expressing anger.

At this point you would probably look at me and ask, "Okay, now what? I'm angry and resentful. My mate is angry and resentful. And our children are in the same condition. What's next?"

Our first step would be to summarize by grouping all of the resentments everyone has expressed into related areas. It is likely that your family members' resentments concerning each particular issue are quite similar, differing only in perspective. Each person in your family must see those different perspectives or viewpoints in order not to view himself or herself as the sole victim.

The Summary

During the previous three hours of our imaginary counseling session, all of your family members have expressed some resentment concerning the blended family system.

Almost every family member has experienced loss. Each one has brought hurt and the fear of experiencing future pain into your blended family system.

Each family member acknowledged feeling a lack of control within the system: The children, over what happens to them and, consequently, their vulnerability; you, the biological parent, over bonding within your family or what happens to your children while they are in their other household; and you, the stepparent, over responsibilities you feel should be yours which remain unassigned because no one seems to want you to step in and take them.

Everyone feels uncomfortable with his blended family roles, or at least with what he thinks they are. You, the stepparent, feel you have a negative image and an undefined role. The children change their birth order as well as their roles depending on which household they are in. And you, the biological parent, often find yourself caught between different roles. Everyone is asking, "Who am I?"

Everyone has to make changes—in the routine of daily living, living accommodations, where he or she works, where he or she goes to school, relationships and the family structure and composition.

Probably everyone in your blended family has held unrealistic expectations at one time or another, and has been disappointed because his or her expectations can't be met.

Your blended family members often find themselves in loyalty conflicts. Sometimes they feel torn between two people. At others, they feel as though they are competing with one family member for the allegiance of another.

Relationships in blended families are almost always points of confusion and conflict. We all want to feel valued as individuals, and often place our value on our position. "How and where do I fit in?" your family members may be asking. With each one struggling to find his or her place, the family lacks real stability.

Bonding and discipline then become major issues.

"Why don't you love my kids?"

"Why don't you discipline your children?"

"I don't have to do what you tell me. You're not my parent."

These common phrases (or battle cries) are heard in blended family households across the nation, not just in yours.

Feelings of loss, sorrow and conflicting loyalties are intensified at birthdays, holidays, graduations, weddings and other family functions.

The resentments your blended family members feel toward the other household often revolve around ex-mates, visitation, holidays and loyalty conflicts between households.

As I have been summarizing in this imaginary therapy session, different members of your family, including the children, have at various times nodded their heads in agreement or made short statements when something struck a particular chord with them. As the summary comes to a close, it's time for the children to be excused from the room.

Letting Go of Resentments

After your children have left the room, it's my turn to ask you a question . . . one of the most important questions that can be asked regarding the well-being of your blended family. Only you and your mate can answer it.

Are you and your mate committed to loving each other and to having a strong Christian marriage?

Some couples sitting in my office at this point say they just don't know.

The wife might say, "It's just been too much and I can't handle it anymore."

The husband may add, "All of this struggling just isn't fair. With everything I have to deal with . . . the system, the loss, her ex, the kids . . . it just isn't fair."

Unfortunately, when we believe something isn't fair, we may decide someone has to pay for it or fix it. In other words, we want our pound of flesh, our revenge. And revenge is counterproductive.

Other couples answer thoughtfully and tearfully, "Yes, we want a strong Christian marriage. We will be committed to loving each other."

How will you answer this question?

What will your mate say?

If your answer is yes, begin by letting go of your resentments.

Do you need to forgive each other for:

- being hypercritical of each other's parenting skills?

- not supporting one another?

- being overbonded or underbonded with the children in your blended family or treating them unfairly?

- not spending enough time together as a couple?

Do both of you need to forgive the children for:

- not working at family bonding?

- some of the hurtful things they've said?

- being rebellious?

- the added stress they have caused in your couple relationship?

Do you need to forgive yourself for:

- "putting your children through a divorce"?

- the ill feelings you have had toward other family members?

- not doing what you know you should do?

- doing what you know you shouldn't?

To be a functional blended family, you have to let go of your resentments. There is no other way. Resentment leads to a prejudiced viewpoint from which you interpret everything. You become oversensitive. Consequently you overreact. Everything becomes exaggerated. Resentment then becomes directed toward situations and the people in those situations.

Forgiveness says, "I'll give you a second chance," and, "I'll cooperate again." For your family to become a healthy blended family, an attitude of forgiveness—a continuous mental position of forgiving—must fill your home. You need to apply forgiveness to yourself as well as extend it to others. It is difficult to move forward in your blended family unless you are willing to forgive and let go of the past, even when the past may mean just yesterday.

At this point, if you really were sitting in my office, I would lead you into prayer. If right now, while you are reading, you have made a decision to forgive your mate, your children, yourself, your ex-mate, your in-laws—whomever you have held resentments against—we invite you to say the following prayer:

> Heavenly Father, I come to You in Jesus' name. As I have been reading I have found that I am angry and resentful. I know that in order for me to help my blended family, I need to be free of these feelings. I give them to You, Lord. Please forgive me for holding onto all of these hurts and resentments and forgive me for who I've been because of them. I am genuinely ashamed of how I have been acting. And Lord, I forgive my family members and everyone in the other household. Although I don't necessarily *feel* loving toward these people right now, I am deciding this very moment no longer to walk in unforgiveness toward them. Help me to be what You want me to be, and please be Lord of my blended family. Amen.

Let's go back to our imaginary counseling session. Now that you and your mate have prayed, it is time to call the children back into the office. As they walk in they wonder what has taken place while they've been gone. As they sit down, I begin talking.

"Your parents have decided that they are going to make this marriage work and they have taken the first step by forgiving each other. Now they have something they would like to say to you."

Then it's your turn. Perhaps you would say something like this:

"We want to have a good marriage, not only for us as a couple, but for you, our children, as well. We know that we won't have a good marriage until we get over our resentments toward each other, and because of that we have just asked for each other's forgiveness. We are giving each other a second chance. We also want to have a happy family. We are going to give our blended family a second chance by asking you to forgive us. Would you please forgive us [or me] for. . . ."

Be very specific as you ask your children's forgiveness. If the children are responsive, I, as the therapist, would work on leading them into forgiving you, as you and your mate forgave each other. Your children need to let go of their resentments, too.

If your children are not responsive, at least they have heard the words. They know how you feel, and where you stand as a couple.

The sooner your family members can let go of past failures and resentments, and put proper structure in place so past mistakes are not repeated, the sooner you can move ahead in building your family life. The longer family members hold onto their failures and resentments, the more overwhelming the work ahead seems, and the more their prospects for successful blended family living diminish.

Who Said It Would Be Easy?

Where does it say family life is supposed to be easy? Many people feel they are failing miserably as a blended family because things are not going smoothly. It is unrealistic to think happy, cohesive families just happen, whether they are nuclear or blended.

If I viewed my work in the same way some people view their blended families, my expectations would be 'way out of line and I would be setting myself up for major disappointments and failure with my self-talk: "I should enjoy, no, love

to go to work every day. I should always be successful.
Every person who walks into my office should get his or her
life straightened out immediately. Everyone should like me.
And everyone should be happy to pay his or her bill.''

If I walked into my office with such an unrealistic attitude,
I would be battered by the realities in which I actually work.
I like my job, but there are days when I would much rather
go fishing. I do not have all of the answers. Some people do
not like me or my counseling style. And people go bankrupt
or refuse to pay their bills. Just because things get difficult at
the office does not mean I am wrong or I should stop going
to work.

By the same token, because things are difficult in your
blended family does not mean you are a failure, you are
wrong or you should stop going home. Although many family tasks in blended families are more difficult than in nuclear
families, you need not throw in the towel and quit.

Certain tasks *are* harder to accomplish in a blended family
than in a nuclear family. They fall into four major categories:
the couple relationship, parenting, family bonding and family identity.

• In a blended family it is more difficult to focus on the
couple relationship since children come with the marriage,
there are one or more ex-mates and other children to relate
to, and finding time for togetherness is hard. But the couple
relationship should not be viewed as less important simply
because it is more difficult to concentrate on in the blended
family. In fact, it must be primary in a family, whether
blended or nuclear, second only to each mate's relationship
with the Lord. It is essential for a husband and wife to establish themselves as a unit apart from all other relationships,
whether with children, extended family members or ex-
mates.

• In nuclear families the children join the family one at a time (unless of course they're twins, triplets, etc.). Mom and Dad have the opportunity, whether or not they take it, to develop complementary *parenting* skills and a united front (the external presentation that the couple cannot be divided). Blended families, on the other hand, are "instant families," allowing no time for the parent and stepparent to develop parenting skills together. A united front is difficult to establish when there has been a longer bond with a biological child than with the new mate. Co-parenting with the other household is an added parenting difficulty for which many blended family couples are totally unprepared.

In past years, the setting of limits and boundaries by both male and female heads of the household (Mom and Dad) was accepted by the children. Today children are less accepting, even in a nuclear family. In a blended family, either the male or the female head of the household is a stepparent, whose parenting is often not accepted by the stepchildren.

Children, however, cannot parent themselves. The biological parents and stepparents are responsible to provide for, nurture, set structure or limitations for and act as role models for their children.

• In a nuclear family, the members belong to only one unit—their nuclear family—and bonding is achieved relatively smoothly. The task of *family bonding* in a blended family is difficult due to alliances with people in other households, alienating alliances within your household, children who move continuously between households and outside influences constantly pushing and pulling at the blended family. However difficult these circumstances are, they do not decrease each family member's need to belong (which after food, water and shelter is the greatest need each human being has). Difficult circumstances do, however, increase the amount of energy that must go into bonding. In a blended family bonding must become a conscious effort.

• Membership in a nuclear family is clear-cut. The first criterion for being a member is biological. The second criterion is residence—nuclear family members usually live in the same household until they go off to college or set up their own residences. The third criterion is legal. Even in adoptive families, both the male and female heads of the household are legally responsible for the children. (This is not true in a blended family.)

With blended families the criteria for membership have to be expanded. Members include those who are permanent residents in your household and those who live there occasionally. To have a sense of *family identity* in a blended family you have to broaden your definition of *family* to include biological and step, custodial and noncustodial.

Remember: Establish yourselves as a couple (making the couple relationship primary) in your blended family. As one of the adults, you have the role of a parent and the responsibilities that go with it. Make a conscious effort to achieve a sense of belonging for every family member, adult or child, step or biological, custodial or noncustodial. Expand your definition of a family to include stepparents, stepchildren and custodial and noncustodial children.

As we conclude our counseling session for the day I ask one more question. And by the way I look around the room, everyone knows I am expecting each one to answer.

My question is: As we work together over the next few sessions (chapters), what are your goals? What do you want to accomplish?

Your answers will probably be similar to the answers I have heard from many blended family members.

We want to:

- accept our blended family status;
- be more accepting of each other;
- treat each other with respect;
- show each other more empathy;
- stop overreacting to circumstances and each other;
- have more patience and tolerance;
- develop a solid marital bond;
- as a couple, make and carry out rules for the home;
- stop viewing disobedience as a personal attack;
- be able to work with the other household for the benefit of the children;
- learn to work with and around the continual shift in household composition.

With those questions and your answers in mind, let's press on together to accomplish the goals you have set for yourself, asking the Lord for His help.

— 7 —

We Are a Family

_____ True or False: You can be loyal to your beliefs
and principles in a nuclear fam-
ily, but you cannot be loyal to
them in a blended family.

That may sound like a ludicrous question, but far too many
people answer this question _true_ by their attitudes and behaviors within the blended family framework.

Eva, a biological parent in a second marriage, has chosen
not to be loyal to her principles.

"In my first marriage I had some pretty clear-cut beliefs
about family life, but all of that went out the window with
my second marriage, to Martin. For example, from the different programs I have heard and the books I have read, I
have concluded that when a child misbehaves, he or she
should be disciplined immediately whenever possible.

"When my children act up and I'm not at home, however,
I do not want Martin correcting them. I want him to wait
until I get there, even if I am gone until late at night with my

job. The problem is, I know my children don't get the immediate feedback they need for their misbehavior. In fact, sometimes they don't get *any* correction. When I get home and hear from Martin how terrible they were all day, I just don't feel like dealing with it. Either I'm too tired or I tell myself that too much time has gone by for consequences to do any real good."

Eva's belief system says, "Discipline children immediately," but she has thrown that belief out. Consequently, her children and family life will suffer. Eva needs to recognize and understand that a cohesive, healthy family life is based on a solid belief system and on principles and guidelines formed out of that belief system.

Before we can be loyal to our values, we need to know what our values are and upon what our belief system is based. One book not only lays out a belief system based on truth, but also offers a strong foundation and role model for family living. That book is the Bible. And even though the Bible doesn't have a blended family role model, per se, it does have a family outline for us to follow.

In some circumstances we can achieve the same result by using different methods. For example, there are various ways to do the dishes. We can wash and dry them as soon as the meal is over. We can soak the dirty dishes in soapy water until we are ready to wash and dry them. We can wash them, rinse them and put them in a rack to air dry. We can load the dishes in a dishwasher, punch a button and put them away at our convenience. All of these approaches will accomplish the same result.

There are some cases, however, where we need to follow very specific steps to ensure the result. During the Christmas holidays last year, Adrienne and Jennifer decided to make candy mints as Christmas gifts. The recipe called for confectioner's sugar, but they mistakenly used granulated sugar. The result? Instead of the smooth, creamy mints they hoped for, the mints were gritty in the mouth and crumbly to the touch. Adrienne and Jennifer told themselves the mints were okay, they were fine, they just had a few minor flaws. Finally they both admitted something was wrong, checked the recipe and discovered their error. The granulated sugar worked up to a point, but following the recipe would have helped to achieve prime results.

Just like doing dishes and making mints, family living requires the performance of specific tasks. Blended families in particular must: put their family structure into place; redefine and build relationships within that structure.

The Bible contains a recipe with a specific plan for putting your blended family structure into place. (See Genesis 2:24; Ephesians 5:22–6:4; Colossians 3:16–21; and 1 Peter 3:1–9.) Just as carefully following the recipe for mints will bring about delicious candy, following this recipe for family living will produce the best results for your blended family. The ingredients are as follows:

• A husband and wife who:

—love each other;

—have become one;

—are submitted to God and to each other;

—accept their roles as parents and the responsibilities that come with those roles.

• A husband who:

—is not harsh with his wife;

—treats his wife with respect;

—is considerate of his wife.

· A wife who:

—submits to her husband;

—respects her husband;

—is considerate of her husband.

· Children who:

—respect,

—honor

—and obey their parents.

· Parents who:

—love,

—teach,

—train,

—nurture,

—provide for

—and manage their children.

· Fathers who do not exasperate their children.

· Family members who:

—are sympathetic, compassionate and humble;

—work to live in harmony;

—do not repay evil with evil, but with blessing.

That, in the condensed version, is the biblical role model for the family. It is the structure set up by God for healthy family living and warm, loving relationships. What in this structure must be changed because you live in a blended family? Let's think it through together.

Do you believe that you and your mate should love each other and be one?

Do you believe that you and your mate should be submitted to God?

Do you believe that each of you should accept your role as a parent and the responsibility that goes with it?

Do you believe that a husband should be considerate of his wife and treat her with respect and not harshness?

Do you believe that a wife should be considerate of her husband, treat him with respect and submit (or adapt herself) to him?

Do you believe that the children in your household, biological and step, should respect, honor and obey their parents?

Do you believe that parents should love, teach, train, nurture, provide for and manage their children?

Do you believe that family members should make every effort to live in harmony?

As you answer these questions honestly you are defining your belief system regarding your family life. Did you or your mate answer no to any of these questions? If so, the topic within the question(s) is probably producing difficulties in your marriage and within your blended family. Whenever we do not follow God's prescription for family living, we are opening ourselves up for problems within our families.

Once you and your mate have clarified your belief system, you can begin putting into place the structure from which your blended family should operate.

What does all of this have to do with conflict?

We have either structure or chaos. When we have chaos we have continual conflict. Look at this example. In our country we have many different structures in place, one of which is related to driving. We are to drive on the right side of the road, obey posted speed limits and other road signs that tell us to stop, yield or slow down. When we approach an intersection we know a red light means stop, a green light means go and a yellow light means yield or caution. Because we accept and obey the rules within that structure, hundreds of thousands of vehicles can travel on the same roads with limited conflict. But when people are not living within the structure conflicts arise.

When I present this concept to biological and stepparents alike, a standard question arises:

"Which comes first, the structure or the emotions?"

The biological parent says unequivocally that emotions come first. "You show me you love my children. Then we'll put this structure into place."

The stepparent responds resoundingly that the structure comes before emotions. "I can't love children who are disrespectful and unruly."

Chaos seldom yields good feelings. In order to limit conflict in your blended family, structure must be put in place. I am not writing this as a biased stepparent. Adrienne, who is a biological parent, and I both believe a biblical family structure is paramount to the success of the family, nuclear or blended.

When we ask you to follow the structure the Bible has so wisely laid out for family living, we assume both you and your mate are emotionally stable. We also assume that neither the biological parent nor the stepparent has an explosive personality disorder, a passive-aggressive personality disorder, a problem with drugs, alcohol, wife or child abuse or pedophilia.

We therefore rule out such questions as, "What do I do when my husband abuses my children or his children physically or sexually? Should I submit to this because the Bible tells me to be a submissive wife?"

Such action on the part of a husband and father is obviously unbiblical, immoral and emotionally and physically unhealthy. Should you submit to your husband's immoral behavior? Absolutely not.

In this book we are addressing people who know and adhere to moral limits and have a common sense awareness of what is right and wrong, healthy and unhealthy. In the above-mentioned case of child abuse, a wife should recognize that her husband is damaging her children, or his, and putting them in life-threatening situations. Her moral common sense, then, enlightened by the Holy Spirit, frees her from rigid obedience to doctrinal law.

What Makes Family Life Healthy?

We have already stated that a cohesive, healthy family life is based on a solid belief system and on principles and guidelines formed out of that belief system and routinely followed. What guidelines, formed out of a biblical belief system, characterize a healthy family?

1. *Family members have a strong Christian orientation.* This orientation provides standards by which members within the family unit can live. Since those standards are not humanistically self-determined, family members know "we all live

by them," even though there are times when those standards run contrary to what we personally want. They are standards determined by a God who is much bigger than we are. All of us, father, mother and children, are required to obey Him.

2. *Family relationships are prioritized appropriately with God first, mate second and children third.* This is basic not only to a healthy family life, but also to a fulfilling couple relationship.

3. *Family members display an ability to show appreciation and to receive compliments from other family members.* Unhealthy families tend to be critical of other members. Critical attitudes breed tension and conflict. In the absence of criticism family members can enjoy being together.

4. *Family members commit their time to being together as a family.* Individual members work out their schedules to be available for planned family functions or spontaneous family fun.

5. *Family members sense a healthy, God-ordered control over their lives.* They view good decision-making (based on their belief system) and hard work, not circumstances and luck, as powerful determinants of their life paths.

6. *Family members are compliant.* They exhibit a basic willingness to follow the program, to be helpful. Household rules (curfew, chores, bedtime, etc.) are logically, reasonably and fairly established on the basis of ethical and moral standards and the superior knowledge and experience of the parents.

7. *Family members talk to one another using good communication skills.* Their tones convey respect. There is an absence of name-calling and derogatory comments. Open and honest with their concerns and emotions, they make sure that listening is as important as talking.

8. *Family members are empathetic toward each other.* They genuinely want to know what other family members are

thinking and feeling. Their empathy communicates, "I respect you," "I value you," "You are important enough to me that I want to understand you."

9. *Family members are committed to the family unit.* Each individual family member sees himself as a part of the team, and is willing to invest himself or herself in the family unit. The byproduct is a healthy sense of belonging.

10. *Family members show their love and affection freely toward one another in verbal, nonverbal and material expressions.* Verbally they express their love, voice their feelings and are willing to self-disclose. Nonverbally they offer affection, moral support and encouragement by attending special events and taking time to do things for other family members. Material expressions of love and affection may include gifts and/ or money.

11. *The family as a unit has good conflict resolution skills.* Whether they are facing an internal problem or an external crisis, family members have confidence in their ability to find and implement solutions to their difficulties, and to come out of crises closer than ever.

As you read through these characteristics describing healthy families, did you find yourself thinking along these lines:

"Sure, those are great guidelines for nuclear families, but they don't have ex-mates to deal with. They don't have to work around noncustodial parents who are either too active and involved or, as in some cases, never around when the children need them. They don't live in small houses with different children coming and going during the week or weekend. They don't have hyperactive stepchildren." And so on, and so on.

Yes, the system of a nuclear family and the suprasystem of

a blended family are very different. And, yes, blended family living includes stresses that nuclear family living does not. Although each of the characteristics listed above will take a concentrated effort on the part of every family member, they can be characteristics that describe your blended family life.

For example, as we stated, healthy families have a strong religious background. Your family may be blending two different church backgrounds. Suppose your children are used to going to the Baptist church while your mate's children went to the Methodist church. You and your mate need to agree on what church you are going to attend as a family, and your children, in time, will adjust.

If your children go to their other household every other weekend, perhaps they will go to the Lutheran church. Or perhaps they won't go to church at all. The other household may even put down your Christian values.

Given these blended family complexities, you will have to work harder to have a strong spiritual foundation. Don't drop your spiritual values as a family in the face of a few obstacles.

In healthy families, family members make time to be together. When you have children living in two households it is clearly difficult to schedule family time.

Have you ever noticed that it doesn't matter if it's 100 degrees and sunny, 10 degrees and snowing, or 50 degrees and raining—if boys want to play football . . . they'll play football? The same principle holds true for any family goal. With a little extra effort and planning, you can find the time or negotiate time with the other household so that your blended family can do things together.

Why is striving for these characteristics so important? For one thing, the family is the most powerful environmental factor in shaping the personality of the child. If we are going to raise healthy children we need healthy families in which to do it. It is true that your children have gone through a divorce. You may feel guilty about that. But for the sake of everyone concerned, these characteristics need to operate within your family.

The divorce rate is higher for second marriages than it is for first marriages, with approximately six out of ten (sixty percent of) remarriages collapsing. As we reported in our book *The Blended Family,* the major cause of divorce in remarriages is child-rearing. In nuclear families, family life is usually a reflection of the couple relationship. In blended families, the couple relationship is most often a reflection of family life.

If you are going to preserve your couple relationship during the turbulent child-rearing years, you cannot just live in the "blended family" status quo. You need to work on developing the characteristics of healthy family life. If you do, you will have healthier children, a healthier couple relationship and a mentally healthier you.

— 8 —
Conflicting Loyalties

"Why do I always end up having to choose sides?"

Wilma sat in tears, thinking about what had transpired that morning. On his way out the door, Wilma's husband, Gary, had told her, "I'd like the boys to get the yard raked. They were supposed to do it last weekend. I want it done tonight before I get home from work."

Forty-five minutes later Wilma overheard her sons talking about getting together for a neighborhood football game right after school. She didn't have the heart to tell them right then that their stepfather wanted the yard raked after school, so she didn't say anything.

Now she was trying to decide who would be the least angry or upset, her husband or her children. She was caught in the middle of a loyalty conflict. If she made the boys rake the yard, they would be upset with her for siding with their stepfather. If she did not, her husband would think she was siding with her children.

This dilemma of conflicting loyalties is commonplace in

blended families and represents the greatest unconscious source of conflict within the suprasystem.

Loyalty in a nuclear family includes not only loyalty to individuals, but also to the family unit as a whole. Not only will competitive brothers jump to each other's defense should an outside party attack, but family members will work hard to keep the family together if some outside force is working against it.

Does loyalty exist in a blended family? Yes, but frequently it is not to every member, and not to the blended family as a unit. The loyalties are generally to relationships where bonding has taken place prior to the remarriage. Some families may even split right down the middle, with Mr. Jones and his children on one side and Mrs. Jones and her children on the other side. Anyone who switches sides is regarded as a traitor. When the children tell different stories about how the living room lamp got broken, she believes her kids and he believes his.

A person who is torn between two individuals who are vying for his or her commitment is in a loyalty conflict. The person caught in the middle sides sometimes with one person and sometimes with the other.

Loyalty conflicts are not limited to blended families. They occur in nuclear families as well, but tend to be more fluid, changing with the issue and the circumstances involved. If the older children in the family are bossy, for example, and usually watch whatever they want on TV, Mom may side with the youngest child every once in a while by letting her watch her favorite program for a change.

In a nuclear family the children occasionally have stronger alliances or closer emotional ties with one parent or the other. These loyalty conflicts are usually transitional and not emotionally explosive. In a blended family, however, loyalty conflicts are more fixed and evoke stronger emotions.

What happens when a child in a healthy nuclear family is upset with Mom (or vice-versa) and runs to Dad with his complaints? More often than not Dad will say, "I know you are upset with Mom right now, but you and I both know she has your best interests in mind. What do you say we go talk to her about it?"

But what happens following a divorce or remarriage when a child goes to Dad complaining about Mom (or vice-versa)? Dad often does not redirect the child back to Mom. Instead he may say, "You're right, son. Your mom *is* hard to get along with."

Triangulations

Who can be caught in a loyalty conflict in a blended family? Just about everybody. Visher and Visher in their book *Old Loyalties, New Ties* (p. 165) identify eight possible loyalty conflict combinations within the blended family suprasystem.

The person at the top of the triangle, in the apex, feels torn between the two people at the bottom of the triangle. The two people at the bottom compete for the allegiance of the person in the apex. Each person at the bottom is saying to the person at the top, "I want you to be committed to me. When you are committed to the other person I am competing with, you are not committed to me."

There are different types of loyalty conflicts.

• *Inner conflict:* One person being torn internally between two others creating an *intrapersonal conflict* for the person in the apex as the two people contend for his or her commitment.

Common Triangulations in Stepfamilies

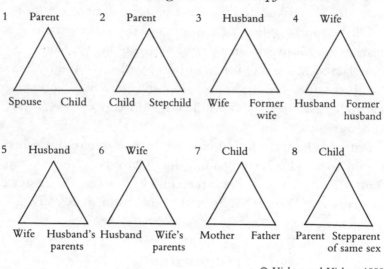

© Visher and Visher, 1988

Relational conflicts: Conflicts that arise within relationships due to a strong loyalty to one of the persons at the bottom of the triangle. The other person at the bottom becomes angry over this loyalty, making it an *interpersonal conflict.*

Consequential conflicts: Conflicts that are inherent to cross-generational loyalties.

Child in the Apex

Following a divorce almost all children experience a loyalty conflict between their mother and father, as in illustration 7. This may not necessarily occur because they are pushed into it, but because Mom and Dad are so upset with each other. If the children form any kind of opinion about the divorce, they may feel as though they are taking sides.

How quickly children are able to resolve this intrapersonal

loyalty conflict regarding their parents is greatly determined by how their parents continue to relate to each other after the divorce and on into a remarriage. If the parents cannot form a working relationship as co-parents, their children's loyalty conflicts may continue into adulthood.

This loyalty conflict, with the child in the apex feeling caught between Mom and Dad, is often intensified at remarriage, depending on the situation. If one parent remarries before the other, the single parent may become upset or angry with the ex-mate, making it difficult for the children even to *act* as if they like the other biological parent. Or the single parent may become fearful of losing his or her children's loyalty, thus working even harder to get more commitment from the children. On the other hand, the parent who is remarrying is focusing on building a new family, and wants the children to be committed to it.

At the remarriage, or even during the dating period, children may experience another type of loyalty conflict. In this conflict the child is still in the apex, but this time he is torn between his parent and his stepparent of the same sex (as his parent), as in illustration 8.

The loyalty conflicts with the child in the apex between Mom and Dad, or between a parent and the same-sex stepparent, are the only ones we had wisdom to address in our first book. Our answer still remains the same.

When children continue to be caught in the apex, it is usually because the adults in their lives are vying for their children's exclusive commitment. And if the adults aren't vying for exclusivity, they are, at the least, competing for the most prominent commitment of their child to them or to their way of thinking and doing things.

To help your children resolve their loyalty conflicts, don't ask for their exclusive commitment. Their commitment to the other parent or same-sex stepparent does not mean they cannot be committed to you. Give your children the permission they need to like, respect, relate to and be part of their other parent's and stepparent's lives.

You may not be aware you are putting your children in a position of having to choose sides. The next time they are disruptive or acting up, ask yourself, "Am I putting my children in the apex of a loyalty conflict?"

Adults in the Apex

One loyalty conflict for adults may be a husband or wife in the apex between his or her mate and parents, as in numbers 5 and 6 in the illustration.

John and Ann are a good example.

"My parents don't like the way John disciplines my children. Every time we get ready to visit my mom and dad, I go through the same thing: Should I try to get Dad and John out doing something together so John isn't around the children much while we are there? Or should I just let John discipline them and pay for it with a nasty phone call from Mom or Dad later?

"When we actually get to my parents' home or when they visit us, instead of taking either route, I find myself jumping on my children's case constantly. If I can keep them in line there will be no need for John to discipline them, and no need for my parents to be angry with me because of John."

To remove herself from the apex of the loyalty conflict between her husband and her parents, Ann needs to say to her parents:

"Mom and Dad, I really appreciate your concern for me and the children, but John and I are going to work out our discipline style together. As my husband and the head of our household, John has to be a part of disciplining the children if we are to have order in our home."

All three aspects of a loyalty conflict are at play in the example you just read. Ann is having an *intrapersonal conflict*. She is torn between loyalty to her parents, whom she knows love her and have her children's best interests at heart, and to her husband, who also loves her and wants the best for her children.

The *interpersonal conflict* comes when there are arguments over John's disciplining or not disciplining the children in front of Ann's parents.

When Ann tells John, "Please don't discipline the children when we are at my parents' house," John feels hurt, angry and betrayed.

"I see. I'm supposed to be a parent at home, but not when we are at your folks'. You expect me to love your children and provide for them, but I'm not supposed to discipline them."

When John *does* discipline the children in front of Ann's parents, they criticize her because "once again, she's allowed John, who's too harsh and dictatorial, to discipline her kids. After all, she *is* their mother!"

Consequential conflicts, inherent to cross-generational loyalties, may come into play if Ann's children overhear or sense that Grandma and Grandpa do not accept John's positional authority. Because of this, John's stepchildren become less accepting of his authority over them at home as well as at their grandparents'.

As in the case of Ann and John, grandparents may find it difficult to accept a new son-in-law or daughter-in-law who will also be a stepparent to their grandchildren. On the other side of the coin are parents who, because they are overly concerned about the well-being of a son or daughter with the added responsibility of stepchildren, put their child in a loyalty conflict.

Your greatest loyalty must be to your mate. When your primary loyalty crosses generations in either direction, to your parents or to your children, you can count on disruptions in your family relationships and your life.

Another loyalty conflict for adults in blended families is with the husband or wife in the apex, torn between his or her current mate and ex-mate, as in illustrations 3 and 4.

Terry, Adelle's husband, had been asking Adelle for two years to take her ex-mate, Gene, back to court for increased child support. As soon as Terry learned the courts had set a specified percent of net income to be paid in child support, he wanted Gene to pay it.

Terry and Adelle went over and over the issue for months, with Terry constantly pointing out to Adelle that the increased child support would allow him to work fewer hours. Then he could spend more time at home, which Adelle wanted him to do.

Then Adelle would explain to Terry again that money was very important to Gene. Taking him back to court for more child support would be like bringing out the heavy artillery, thus creating more emotional turmoil for her and the children than the money was worth.

Adelle was caught in the middle between her husband and her ex-mate. Should she take Gene back to court and make her husband happy, or should she let the child support remain the same and keep her ex-mate happy?

When Adelle finally tired of the conflict, she made an appointment with her pastor. He thought taking Gene back to court was both logical and biblical. Logically, Terry could cut back his hours and spend more time at home, which would improve their family life. Biblically, if the court set a specified amount to be paid in child support by the biological father of Adelle's children, it was Gene's responsibility to pay that amount. After the conversation with her pastor, Adelle eventually took Gene back to court.

Adelle and Terry had a solid couple relationship. Adelle stated, and Terry agreed, that she had no feelings of affection for Gene. But she found it difficult to be disloyal to Gene in her loyalty to Terry.

There are several reasons why a husband or wife may find himself or herself in the apex between a current mate and an ex-mate. First, an individual in the apex may not have divorced emotionally from a former mate. Like Cyndee, he or she may still be seeking the ex-mate's approval.

"I know this is silly, but I just want my ex to say, 'Hey, Cyndee, you're okay.' And although I know it will probably never happen, I want to know that I'm an okay person in his eyes."

Secondly, a person who finds himself or herself in the apex of this particular loyalty conflict may see the ex-mate as a dependent personality who needs him or her. Even though he or she is not in love with the ex, nor could ever live with him or her again in a husband/wife relationship, he or she believes the ex-mate will fall flat without his or her support. This belief may lead a noncustodial parent to visualize all kinds of negative consequences for his or her noncustodial children if this would ever actually happen: "If I don't run over and fix the furnace, the children will freeze."

Other individuals who find themselves in this particular loyalty conflict may have absolutely no positive feelings whatsoever for an ex-mate. But even fear or hostile feelings can create an emotional connectedness to an ex-mate, which in turn can create a loyalty conflict within the marriage. "If I do what my husband/wife wants me to do, my ex will try to turn the children against me. He may want more court-ordered visitation or even go for custody of the children just as a way to get back at me."

There will always be disharmony in the couple relationship when a previous couple relationship is elevated (or viewed as equal), for whatever reason, above the current marital relationship. The current marital relationship, which includes the feelings of your mate, must have your primary loyalty.

One of the loyalty conflicts for adults within a blended family may be a parent caught in the middle between a biological child and a stepchild, as in illustration 2.

Biological parents, particularly noncustodial fathers, may struggle over giving time and affection to stepchildren who live with them when they feel guilty over not being able to have the same kind of daily relationship with their noncustodial children. They may feel they are betraying their biological children if they bond with their stepchildren. On the other hand, they may feel they are betraying their stepchildren if they assume the role of parent only when their biological children come over on weekends.

This loyalty conflict can be summed up by the phrase "You feel guilty if you do and guilty if you don't." Biological parents feel guilty if they love their children more than their stepchildren. And because biological parents have an underlying desire to get the message across to their children that no other relationship will be a threat to their relationship, they feel guilty if they love their stepchildren as much as they love their children.

Orin, a biological father, felt torn between his daughter and his two stepchildren. He was constantly worrying about keeping everything even and fair between them. Whenever Orin referred to the children in his household he called all of them his children and never referred to his stepchildren as "my stepchildren." One afternoon shopping when Orin introduced the children to a co-worker, his biological daughter burst into tears.

As Orin was tucking his daughter into bed that evening he asked, "Sandra, whatever was wrong at the store today? One minute you were fine. The next minute you were crying. What happened?"

"You introduced all of us as your children. You always say they are your children. They are *not* your children. They are your stepchildren. *I'm* your child. Me. Sandra."

The most common loyalty conflict in blended families is with the parent in the apex, caught between the current mate and the children, as in illustration 1.

As stated previously, the number-one cause of divorce in remarriages is child-rearing. As we have talked to couples around the country, it is evident that child-rearing is "the issue." When we ask biological parents about child-rearing issues, they all give basically the same answer.

"My mate says I'm always choosing my children over him. My children complain that I never stick up for them. I feel trapped, torn; some days I just want out."

Clearly biological parents have a longer and, at least in the early stages of remarriage, deeper bond with their children than with their new mate. We're not asking biological parents to give up the parent/child bond, but, to quote Visher & Visher in *Old Loyalties, New Ties* (p. 165), "Family relationships are likely to be disturbed if the primary coalition is between two generations."

Marital and family life suffer even in a nuclear family when a parent and child continue in a coalition against the other parent. This is not the natural order God intended for healthy, functioning families. Children feel no need to accept a stepparent when they receive their biological parent's primary loyalty. If you want your children to accept their stepparent, you need to let them know your primary loyalty is to your mate.

If you show your children you value and honor your mate, it helps them have a positive view of their stepparent. It also keeps them from being prima donnas (or dons) and puts the adults in control of the family, not the children.

Making the couple relationship primary does not mean all of your energy and emotions are directed toward your mate to the exclusion of your children. Loyalty does not have to be either/or.

Jordan decided to put his dad's loyalty to the test. Right before time to leave for his soccer game, Jordan told his dad he did not want his stepmom to come to his game. He wanted it to be "me and you, just like it was before you married Laura."

Dad calmly told Jordan, "Jordan, I have been looking forward to your soccer game all week, picturing Laura and me sitting together rooting for you, cheering you on. I want to share this experience with both of you."

This father quickly let his son know loyalty was not going to be an either/or situation. He identified his loyalty to Jordan by attending his soccer game as an avid fan. His expression of loyalty to his son, however, was going to include the opportunity for his new wife to participate as well.

Self in the Apex

Yet another triangulation exists, with you in the apex, torn between others' wants and your values and responsibilities. You will find yourself caught in the other triangulations frequently unless this conflict is resolved.

When we are in a loyalty conflict, it is difficult to identify

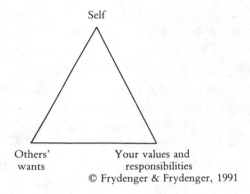

Self

Others'   Your values and
wants   responsibilities
© Frydenger & Frydenger, 1991

our values. Why? Because loyalty issues are the greatest unconscious source of conflict in blended families. We become
so caught up in "Should I get on track with person A or with
person B?" that taking the time to sort out our values and
responsibilities goes by the wayside. Before getting on track
with anyone, we need to get on track with our own values
and responsibilities.

When the wants and desires of the two people at the bottom of the triangle conflict with each other, they try to draw
the person in the apex over to their side or their way of
thinking. If the person in the apex has not defined his values,
he will find himself making decisions based on relationship
rather than on morals and logic. After he has defined his
values and stated his position, one or both of the individuals
vying for his allegiance may get angry. Their anger is not
because he has chosen one person over another, however, but
because he is remaining true to what he believes.

Jim felt his ten-year-old stepson, Scottie, should be in bed
by 9:00 every night in order to get enough rest and give his
parents some quiet time of their own in the evenings. Scottie
had different ideas about how much sleep he needed. He

hated to go to bed "that early": He might miss something really important!

Dinah, Scottie's mother, had never really decided on an "official" bedtime. She would start telling Scottie at 8:30 to think about getting ready. Periodically, then, she would yell at Scottie to get his pajamas on and finally, around 10:00 or 10:30, Scottie would get to bed.

When Jim explained to Dinah why he thought Scottie should be in bed at 9:00, she came up with several excuses why he should be allowed to stay up: a good TV program was coming on, Scottie was not tired yet or he needed time to wind down.

Some nights Jim would start watching the clock angrily at nine, then become irate by ten when Scottie still wasn't in bed. Other nights Scottie was in bed by nine, which made *him* very unhappy. Every night Dinah felt guilty.

One morning over coffee with friends, Dinah mentioned Jim's insistence that Scottie get to bed by nine. Dinah was challenged to clarify her values when her friend Jane asked her, "Dinah, don't you feel it's your parental responsibility to see that Scottie gets an adequate amount of sleep?" At that point Dinah realized it was not only reasonable but responsible for her to get Scottie to bed at nine.

Even so, she worried. "Now that I've decided Scottie should be in bed by nine, it seems like I'm agreeing with my husband. What is my son going to think about that?"

Many individuals in the apex, particularly when caught between a child and a mate, discover that when they define their values, they usually line up with the values of the other adult in their household, not their children.

If the person in the apex asks, "*Who* am I going to commit to?," instead of, "*What* am I going to commit to?," there will always be problems. You can remain loyal to everyone in your family, even when standing up for your values means you are not aligning yourself with a particular individual.

In summary, the couple relationship must be the strongest coalition for both the husband and the wife. The couple's loyalty to each other must surpass cross-generational loyalties to either children or parents and must surpass former marital relationships if a healthy blended family is to emerge.

Identify your values and your responsibilities. Then you can live out what Jesus said in John 8:31–32: ". . . If you hold to my teaching, you are really my disciples. Then you will know the truth, and the truth will set you free."

If two people are vying for your allegiance follow these steps:

1. Stop and remove yourself from the debate.
2. Look at the issues.
3. Identify your values and responsibilities relating to that issue.
4. Decide your position based on your values and responsibilities.
5. State your position and support it (biblically, if necessary).

After making your decision in step 4, go to your mate and identify your position. If you and your mate agree, great. If not, you will have to practice conflict resolution skills (which will be discussed in the next chapter) in order to come to a solution acceptable by both parties.

When an agreement has been reached, calmly, warmly but matter-of-factly state your decision to the other party(ies)— your children, your parents or your former mate. You and your mate can be in the room together while a position is being stated, but the person in the apex should address the other party(ies) while the mate listens quietly.

Two interrelated issues often distract blended family members from sticking to their values. These are loyalty, which we've discussed in this chapter, and conflict resolution, which we will disucss in the next chapter.

— 9 —
Resolving Conflict

"Living in a blended family is like walking on eggshells all the time."   —a blended family mother

What an awful feeling when the tension in your house is so thick your muscles tense up at the base of your skull or you experience heart palpitations and tightness in your chest simply because two family members are in the same room at the same time!

Family therapists note that conflict arises during times of transition such as marriage, childbirth, adolescence, empty nest, divorce and remarriage, and changes in the household composition. This being the case, blended families have an open door to conflict. Not only do they go through the traditional stressful stages of life, but their homes are always in a state of transition.

Since conflict situations are inevitable in the nuclear or blended family, family members who dread conflict will always be disappointed and frustrated. The difficulty lies less in the issues that generate the conflict than in whether or not we resolve the conflict, how long it takes to resolve it and how much damage is done before we do, *if* we do.

Some families seem to face problems with little or no tension between family members. They take the time to talk things over and work as a team to solve problems quickly. They look at a problem, evaluate it, search out possible solutions, decide what steps to take to resolve it and commit to that decision as a family.

Other families turn even the most mundane differences into strife and conflict. When a conflict arises they immediately move into opposite corners as they blame, criticize and either become silent or "talk at" the other person(s).

Susan Heitler, Ph.D., in her book *From Conflict to Resolution* (p. 5), defines conflict as "a situation in which seemingly incompatible elements exert force in opposing or divergent directions." When we discussed loyalty conflicts in the previous chapter, we were talking about two people who were putting someone else in the middle while conflicting with each other in opposing or divergent directions.

In this chapter we want to look at how two or more people with opposing or diverse interests deal with each other. Wilma, in the opening scene of chapter 8, felt caught in a loyalty conflict between her sons and her husband over a family chore. Had Wilma's husband, Gary, told his stepsons before he went to work that he wanted the yard raked when he came home, he would have left Wilma out of the conflict. It would then have been up to Gary and the boys to resolve their difference.

Conflict exists where people think it exists, whether or not there are opposing issues. As long as two or more ideas, needs or desires are *perceived* to oppose each other, there is conflict. Tension grows between family members when a problem, be it real or perceived, is not being addressed, when poor management skills are being utilized or when someone is seen as being disloyal.

During stressful times, healthy families tend to work as a team because of their high level of loyalty to the family unit. They trust the skills and motives of other family members to resolve the conflict in a mutually satisfying manner.

Blended families often do not have this high level of loyalty to the family unit. Instead of operating from a team concept, each family member may be out for himself or herself or his or her faction of the family. While they could be thinking in terms of "we" by asking such questions as "What do we as a family want?" or "What are our interests as a family?" they may instead be thinking in terms of "I." "What do I want?" "What are my interests?" The switch from a team-centered orientation to a self-centered orientation means that the best you can get, in terms of conflict resolution, is second-best.

Cooperation is a necessary element in resolving conflicts satisfactorily. The question, then, is, "Am I going to take an oppositional stance or am I going to cooperate?" Are you trying to cooperate with your mate? Are you trying to co-operate with the children? Are you trying to cooperate with your parents and stepparents? Are you trying to cooperate with the other household? At this point, the question is *not,* "Are they trying to cooperate with me?"

Conflict has three aspects: conflict content, conflict process and conflict results.

Conflict content is the subject matter over which you are disagreeing. For example, "What should we have for sup-per?" Some family members may want steak, other family members may want spaghetti, and if you have a large family, still others may want chicken. The conflict content, in this situation, is what your family is going to eat for supper.

The *conflict process* is how you deal with your differences.

Once you have identified a difference of opinion, how are you going to go about resolving that difference? Some people argue while others withdraw. Some people give in and some people want to talk it out. Some people complain while others attack insistently and incessantly. Some processes improve the situation while others only make it worse.

The *conflict results* are the outcome of the conflict process. Is one party happy? Are both parties happy? Or is everybody unhappy because the family's poor conflict resolution skills have prevented any satisfactory results?

When you can't resolve a conflict issue, is it because of the content or the process? Frequently it is because of the process. A bad process often adds to content problems.

Conflict Styles

As you look back at different conflicts in which you have been involved, were you sometimes cooperative and at other times oppositional? Do you have a tendency to deal with conflict in a certain way or style?

Numerous personality inventories and models demonstrate how various personality types face conflict. Here are the five major types of personalities in conflict that we have gleaned from our research, counseling and seminar experience, and even within our own family.

The five types are: the escape artist, the dominator, the peacekeeper, the deal maker and the team builder.

As you read through the descriptions of these five types, not only will you see which one you use most often, but you will also discover which style your mate, your children, your stepchildren and your ex-mate use most often. While going through the characteristics of each style, consider how the interplay between your style and your mate's style may be keeping your house in more turmoil than the normal content problems of a blended family merit.

The Escape Artist

This person does not deal with conflict. If there is an argument in the kitchen, he will stay in the bedroom. If conflict breaks out he may go for a walk, a drive in the car or even a respite at the Holiday Inn.

If there is a conflict at home, the stepdad who is an escape artist may start working longer hours at the office. When he does get home, his stepchildren are already in bed. The noncustodial parent escape artist might stop seeing his or her children because working out visitation with the ex-mate is just too much of a hassle.

The escape artist believes that most conflict situations cannot be resolved. The bottom line for the escape artist is: "I can't win. Why get involved?" Rather than risk conflict, he will stay away from it altogether. By doing so, he also avoids appearing as though he has chosen sides.

The Dominator

Dominators are concerned most about their own interests and goals. They may be dictatorial or they may mask their domination as maternalism or paternalism, but when push comes to shove, dominators get what they want. Their philosophy? "In every conflict someone will get his way. I'm going to be that someone."

If some family members want to go to Florida for a vacation and some family members want to go to California, but the dominator wants to go to Colorado, he or she will fight, argue, threaten, cajole, coerce and manipulate until everybody else has surrendered.

Dominators can best be described as large, high-powered

locomotives. If you want to get on track with them, they are glad to have you aboard. But if you are standing in the middle of the track, they will run you down.

The Peacekeeper

Peacekeepers want everyone to get along. They will take whatever steps are necessary—even self-sacrificing ones—to protect relationships and keep conflict at a minimum. Their conflict philosophy is, "I'll give in. That way you will love me."

The Deal Maker

Deal makers hope to negotiate a compromise between what appear to be irreconcilable differences. Their philosophy is, "In order for everyone to be happy, we all have to give a little."

Deal makers believe that they need to give up something to get what they want. "I'll go to your mother's for Thanksgiving, even though I don't want to, if you'll go to my mother's for Christmas." Or, "I'll stop yelling at your children, even though they need it, if you'll stop yelling at my children." Unfortunately, deal makers often try to make up for the ground they lost in the last compromise, thus making relationships strained, cool and defensive.

The Team Builder

Team builders like to get everyone involved in defining the problem and making the decision. They sincerely believe that "two heads are better than one." They regard conflict resolution not only as a way to find the answer to problems, but also as a means to strengthen relationships.

Team builders believe that everyone can win if they all take the time to talk openly and honestly with one another. By practicing cooperation, team builders are able to commit, and gain the commitment of others, in finding and using mutually satisfying solutions.

To show how each of these types works in a given situation, let's imagine that you have come over to my house to help me work on my yard. We have worked for two hours straight in 95-degree, central Illinois, high-humidity heat. We are both dying of thirst, but neither one of us has voiced our need. I know there is only one can of Coke in my refrigerator, and I really like Coke.

If I am an escape artist, I won't mention being thirsty; neither will I mention that there is a Coke in my refrigerator. I do not want to risk conflict, and I hope and pray you will not mention being thirsty either. When we have finished the job I'll thank you, outside, waving goodbye with a friendly "See you later."

If I am a dominator, we will walk into the house, I will open the refrigerator, pop the top off the Coke and gulp it down. As I set the empty can on the counter I will look at you and ask, "Would you like something to drink?"

If you answer, "Yeah, I'll take one of those," I will reply, looking back into the refrigerator, "Gee, that must have been the last one. How about some iced tea?"

If I am a peacekeeper, once we are in the kitchen I will ask if you would like to have a Coke. If your answer is yes, I will give you my last Coke with a smile on my face and resentment in my heart, thinking, *Why didn't he offer me part of that? He should have known that was my last Coke. Why else would I be drinking water?*

If I am a deal maker, I will offer you the Coke. If you say you want it, I will tell you there is only one Coke, which we will have to share. Then I will get out two glasses the same size and add ice only after painstakingly pouring in perfectly even amounts. (Icecubes, being different sizes, could change the amount of Coke I am so carefully dividing.) All the while I am drinking my half of the Coke, I am thinking, *I could have had the whole thing if he had just gone home.*

If I am a team builder, I will get all of my cards on the table right away.

"I'm thirsty. Are you thirsty?"

If your answer is yes I will continue, "All I have in the house to drink is water and one can of Coke. And Coke is what I am really thirsty for. What are you thirsty for?"

If you reply, "I'd really like to have a Coke, too," we will talk over how to satisfy our desire for a big glass of ice-cold Coke.

"Let's see, we could share the one in the refrigerator."

"Or we could go to the store and buy a carton."

"What about that fast-food place down the road? We could drive through and pick up two extra-large Cokes to go. Which may not be a bad idea considering the way we look."

"Hey, we could drive over to my house. I have a liter of Coke in my refrigerator. We could even make a float with the vanilla ice cream I've got in my freezer."

There is an appropriate time to use each of these five conflict styles. Different situations call for different approaches.

Sometimes Christians think Jesus taught only peacekeeping because He said, "If someone strikes you on one cheek, turn to him the other also. If someone takes your cloak, do not stop him from taking your tunic" (Luke 6:29). Actually, though, Jesus used them all.

When people in the synagogue were going to throw Him over the cliff after He read the Isaiah account (as recorded in Luke 4), Jesus escaped conflict by walking away. When He walked into the Temple and overturned the moneychangers' tables, Jesus dominated. When the soldiers came to appre-

hend Him in the Garden of Gethsemane, Jesus kept peace.
When He was asked to pay taxes, Jesus paid with a Roman
coin removed from a fish's mouth, saying, "Give to Caesar
what is Caesar's, and to God what is God's" (Matthew
22:21b). He struck a balanced deal. When the Pharisees were
preparing to stone a woman caught in adultery, Jesus exhib-
ited team building. By the time everyone had left that situation they had all won!

There is no right or wrong style for dealing with conflict.
You can, however, choose the wrong style for a particular
conflict situation. Or you can get stuck using the same style
over and over again. Most of us use one of these five styles
repeatedly because we learned it in childhood. The style you
learned to use for resolving conflict might have been adequate in your family of origin. It might have worked fairly
well in your previous nuclear family. It might not work in
your blended family due to the complexity of the blended
family system.

Team Building: The Best Choice

The one style that is clearly the most effective in building
a sense of family is team building. This is a process. For that
process to work, you must be a team builder. To be a team
builder, you must cultivate the following attitudes about
your approach to people and to conflict:

1. A team builder values other people. He or she believes
others have a right to their own opinions. He or she is not
only willing to listen to the opinions of others, but genuinely
wants to know more about them.

2. The team builder accepts people's differences of opinion. He recognizes that those differences are not necessarily

right or wrong, but are based on each individual's perception of the conflict.

3. The team builder views these differences not only as being starting points for conflict resolution, but also as providing the healthy variety of thought necessary to creative decision-making.

4. A team builder is able to identify assertively his own goals and interests. He has thought through personal wants, having ruled out irrational thinking. He feels comfortable, therefore, in expressing his position.

5. The team builder wants to involve all conflicting parties in the resolution process.

6. Once everyone has expressed his or her initial position, the team builder is willing to cooperate in the process of resolving the conflict.

7. The team builder is willing to accept momentary consequences (for example, the amount of time required or temporary discomfort in the relationship) in order to build a good working relationship.

8. A team builder recognizes that being trustworthy and being able to trust are necessary for cooperation.

9. A team builder does not use coercion, manipulation or force to get what he wants, but tries to persuade by discussing all of the information presented rationally.

10. The team builder will commit to the consensus of the group.

One of the biggest advantages of team building is that it builds a sense of family through understanding, acceptance and cooperation. Each time the family resolves a situation in this manner, more trust between family members and more confidence in the family unit as a whole result.

Conflict Resolution Skills

Conflict in the home changes everyone's behavior. Family members do and say things they regret later. There have undoubtedly been moments when you could not believe how you were acting in the heat of conflict.

How do you and other members in your family change this negative pattern? By changing the conflict process—learning to resolve conflict through team building.

Relationships in a family are long-term. You will deal with your mate, your children and stepchildren for the rest of your life. You will also deal with your children's other biological parent and the other household one way or another for the rest of your life. In order to relate successfully to all of the people in your blended family suprasystem, you need to practice conflict resolution skills that have a positive long-term effect, build the relationship and produce mutually satisfying solutions.

In *From Conflict to Resolution* (p. 22) Susan Heitler, Ph.D., identifies the three key stages in conflict resolution as:

1. Expression of initial position;
2. Exploration of underlying concerns;
3. Selection of mutually satisfying solutions.

In *Getting Together, Building Relationships As We Negotiate* (pp. 9–12), Roger Fisher and Scott Brown list six fundamental ways to deal with differences:

1. Balance reason with emotion.
2. Gain clear understanding.
3. Utilize good communication skills.
4. Be reliable by using trustworthy behavior.

5. Use persuasion and not coercion.
6. Practice mutual acceptance.

Other earlier theories have identified seven key ways to resolve conflict:

1. Clarify issues.
2. Reduce broad issues to manageable units.
3. Increase empathy.
4. Reduce hostility.
5. Identify goals.
6. Rank goals.
7. Establish conflict resolution steps to take as soon as a conflict arises.

Heitler identified three stages in conflict resolution. Fisher and Brown list six fundamental qualities for dealing with differences, while previous negotiation theories identified seven elements for resolving conflict. Frydenger & Frydenger, after mixing these all together, have devised seven stages of conflict resolution, which include basic qualities and key elements:

1. Define the conflict.
2. State your position.
3. Identify underlying concerns.
4. Practice active listening skills.
5. Create possible solutions.
6. Select mutually satisfying solutions.
7. Commit to the solutions decided upon.

1. *Define the problem.* Too many families know "something is wrong," but fail to confront the problem. They just

live with the conflict. Some suppress it, letting it come out in passive-aggressive behavior. Some family members expect others to be mindreaders. Still other family members drop hints or allude to "a problem."

When you are in a conflict, express it explicitly and in its early stages. Once family members begin to admit honestly that they are indeed at odds with one another, they may find multiple issues at play. Often a peacekeeper or an escape artist will let issues build up into an emotional arsenal before one short fuse blows them all out in the open. Even if that's the case, always address only one issue at a time.

2. *Each individual states his or her position.* Stating a position means telling other family members how you feel about the conflict issue as you enter the conflict. Before stating your position, think it through, formulate your ideas and be able to articulate clearly how you feel to other family members. "That's just the way I feel about it" and "I want to do this because I *want* to" are not acceptable opening position statements.

As Fisher and Brown advise, "Balance rational thinking and emotions." We cannot enter into conflicts without emotion, but our emotion must be balanced with rational thinking.

3. *Identify underlying concerns (interests).* In this stage the family begins to look nonjudgmentally at the positions of everyone involved. It is imperative that individuals switch their thinking from "It's either going to be your idea or my idea" to looking for ways to utilize or blend one or more ideas. Genuinely increasing your empathy toward the positions of other family members will reduce their hostility toward your position, as well as hostility in general. Such empathy requires good communication skills.

4. *Practice active listening skills.* A good communicator

knows communication is a two-way street, involving both talking and listening.

When you are speaking, speak for yourself. Practice integrity. Say what you mean, and mean what you say. Use "I" messages: "I feel (angry) when you (come home late) because (I think you don't care)." Avoid using "you" messages that serve only to blame, criticize and create ill feelings: "You never do what I ask you to do."

When you are listening, listen actively to what the other person is saying instead of planning your next rebuttal statement. Help the other person explore his or her feelings by asking questions or interjecting short statements paraphrasing what he or she just said. By so doing you say, "I hear you."

5. *Create possible solutions.* When you genuinely listen to the concerns of other family members and state your own position accurately, you will be surprised to discover you often share the same concern. Up until that point, everyone has been trying to create a solution with a limited perspective. Creating solutions to a conflict is much easier once you have a complete picture of the existing circumstances and feeling levels.

The effort invested in resolving a conflict will be most profitable when all possible solutions are proposed. Take your time in the "create-a-solution" stage. Don't present just a few ideas and then quit. Remember, your goal is to come up with the best possible solution for everyone involved.

6. *Select mutually satisfying solutions.* Select the solutions that best meet the concerns of all parties. Then all can leave the session satisfied with the solutions because they had a part in creating and selecting those solutions.

7. *Commit to the solutions.* Commitment can come only when the conflict resolution produces a feeling of closure for

everyone. All members should be able to say, "I'm glad that's finally settled."

The time and effort put into resolving a conflict are wasted if all the individuals involved in the conflict are not committed to following through with their end of the resolution. You may strike the perfect deal, but if some family members refuse, whether actively or passively, to keep their word, the resolution is of little value.

As a family you may have resolved, for example, that everyone is to make his or her bed before going to work or school or suffer a consequence that evening. If you sneak home from work on your lunch hour to make your children's beds because you don't want them to suffer any consequences, neither you nor your children are keeping your end of the resolution. And your mate might ask justifiably, "What's the point?"

How Does It Work?

Josh and Marie have identified that they want their three teenagers to be home by 9:30 on weekdays and midnight on weekends. Curfew had previously been a point of conflict for them, but, through several sessions of team building, they came to a mutually satisfying agreement. How?

During a family meeting, Josh and Marie stated how they felt about the children's curfew. Their teenage children then stated their unified position: "We should be allowed to stay out until 10:30 on weeknights and 1:00 or 1:30 on weekends. That's what time all the other kids have to be home."

The vote is three to two, three saying curfew should be 10:30 P.M. on weekdays and 1:00 or 1:30 A.M. on weekends, two saying curfew should be 9:30 P.M. on weekdays and midnight on weekends. If team building is the goal, what should Josh and Marie do in this case? Should the majority rule?

Listening to children share their views and feelings is an excellent way to build parent-child relationships. Don't ever forget, however, that you are the parents and they are the children. Parents are wiser and more experienced than children, and are responsible for setting appropriate limitations in their lives.

Certain things are not negotiable and one of them is curfew—except, perhaps, in special situations such as homecoming, prom and graduation. Even on special occasions curfew needs to be matched with your children's ages, maturity levels and the supervision provided.

As you work through this conflict resolution process, you will begin to recognize the different conflict styles as they arise.

The escape artist in your family will be quiet during family discussions, if he or she has not already found an excuse to be absent. He or she will be unwilling to acknowledge that there is a conflict and equally unwilling to find a solution.

The dominator will try relentlessly to push his or her solution through.

The peacekeeper will say whatever you want him or her to say. He or she will agree with everybody. If that does not ease the tension, he or she will take the blame for everything and recommend that forgiving and forgetting be the rule.

The deal maker will note that he has some losses in this arrangement, and will want to get back to the bargaining table as soon as he can to regain them.

If you find yourself falling into one of these categories, reread the attitudes of the team builder until you have them almost memorized. Then practice being a team builder until it comes naturally.

As you work at team building with family members who

have different conflict resolution styles, you may find you need to be quiet awhile and wait for the escape artist to talk about how he or she feels. Or you may need to engage him or her actively in the conversation by asking questions and pointing out that everyone can be pleased with the solution.

Work at strengthening the peacekeeper, thus helping him or her feel more confident in expressing opinions. "Don't tell me what you think *I* think, tell me what *you* think about this situation."

Stand up to the dominator. Do not let him or her run over you or the rest of the family. Do not be afraid to remind the dominator, "You are trying to dominate again. This is team-work." Be willing to let the dominator get angry with you; you can count on it if things are not going his or her way. (It has always worked in the past!)

Remind the deal maker not to rush to resolve the next issue in order to make up for anything he might lose in this one. Point out tactfully that it takes time to look at all the possible solutions and you want to take that time.

Remember, team building works best when everyone is willing to cooperate. Reciprocity pays. Niceness begets niceness. Cooperation promotes cooperation. Reliability brings about more reliability. Trust cultivates more trust. Loyalty gives rise to more loyalty. That is the way it works in God's framework for human relationships.

— 10 —

Co-Parenting

"Mom, why can't Tina and Jerry help with the dishes once in a while? Linda and I have other things to do, too, you know."

Who did the dishes, and when, had become a nightly battle in the Gregory household. When Les and Karen married, they each had custody of their two teenage children. Karen's children were accustomed to doing family chores; Les' children were not. After several weeks of listening to arguments over who had K.P. duty, Karen and Les made specific plans for the evening meal preparation and clean-up.

Since Karen was working second shift, Les would prepare the meal and the children would take turns doing the dishes and cleaning up the kitchen. On the nights his stepchildren were to do the dishes, Les would continue to remind them until the job was done.

But on the first few nights Les' children were to do the dishes, they waited until their stepsiblings were out of the room before turning on the sob stories for Dad.

"Dad, I have to get a four-page report in tomorrow and I haven't even started!"

"And I have to call Susie about my science assignment. I left my science book at school and she has to give me the questions to study for the test."

Ninety percent of the time, Les ended up doing the dishes for his children because they always had more important things to do.

What did Les teach the children in his home? He taught his biological children they really didn't have to be responsible. He sent the message "To get out of doing things in life, just moan and groan and manipulate."

Simultaneously, Les taught his stepchildren that life isn't fair, manipulation works and rules were made to be broken. And he communicated to his wife his unreliability and failure to keep his word. Karen believed she and Les were working on a discipline plan together and that both of them were fully intent on carrying it out. In reality, Karen was working on a discipline plan and Les was doing his own thing regardless of what he and Karen had agreed upon.

As a parent, what are you trying to accomplish with your children? Discipline and limit-setting should do more than keep children out of trouble: They should help them develop lifestyles that will benefit them in the years to come.

Is the way you interact with the children in your household beneficial for them? Will it produce the kind of traits and qualities you want to instill in your children? Or are you, like Les, interacting with the children in your household so as to instill negative character traits that may hinder them later in life?

Biological and stepparents often manifest marked differences in their approaches to discipline. These differences can destroy the marital relationship or the blended family unit

. . . or both. But when the husband and wife use the collaborating techniques of team building to discipline the children in their blended family, they are co-parenting.

The prefix *co* means "with, together, jointly" and "one that is associated in an action with the other." When we co-parent, therefore, we parent "with" our mates. We parent "jointly," "in association with" our mates, not in opposition.

Leniency vs. Harshness

Interaction with children in some blended families, whether initiated by the biological parent or the stepparent, may not have an identifiably healthy goal. It is unhealthy for the children when biological parents block natural and logical consequences for their children's misbehavior. It is equally unhealthy for the children when stepparents overemphasize punishment or drip with resentment toward their stepchildren.

If these parental reactions are so unhealthy for the children, why is the biological parent often lenient and the stepparent just as often harsh?

Sometimes our parenting styles are simply the outgrowth of our personalities and/or how we were parented. At other times our parenting styles may be reactionary responses to the blended family system.

Biological parents may exhibit too-lenient parenting styles for one or a combination of the following reasons: guilt, loyalty conflicts, fear of loss and reaction to the stepparent's harshness.

Guilt

As we mentioned previously, biological parents often feel guilty for subjecting their children to a divorce, regardless of who wanted the divorce. Some biological parents may spend the rest of their lives trying to compensate for the divorce by being too lenient with their children, though they will seldom define it that way.

It is also common for biological parents to experience guilt over spending time with a new mate. Consequently they may become lax in setting limits for their children.

Noncustodial parents who see their children a few days a week or less may attempt to make up for the loss of the daily parent/child relationship and their feelings of guilt by giving their children almost anything they want, within and without reason.

Conflicting Loyalties

Conflicting loyalties are a major reason for biological parents' unwillingness to co-parent by following through with a discipline program. When imposing consequences for misbehavior they may feel they are being disloyal to their children. Until biological parents have a clear understanding of their parental duties and child-rearing goals they will be unable to disengage from loyalty conflicts. Only then can they separate wanting to make their children happy at all costs from doing what is best for their children through co-parenting.

Fear of Loss

The fear of losing their children's loyalty to the other household is an ever-present threat for some biological parents. This loss may be acted out in actual living arrangements or as children align themselves emotionally and psychologically with the other household. Biological parents in this situation fear that being strict will drive their children to prefer living in the ex-mate's home.

Reaction to Stepparent's Harshness

Biological parents are often too lenient because they feel the stepparent is too harsh. They try to balance that harshness by going overboard on empathy, understanding and exceptions to the rules.

At the same time the biological parent is working to balance the stepparent's harshness, the stepparent is often trying to balance the biological parent's leniency. This is a primary example of parenting in opposition instead of cooperation.

Many stepparents are looking out for the long-term interests of their stepchildren. They believe that teaching a child to follow the rules and be respectful is far more important than making the child happy. When they see the biological parent consistently making excuses for a child or accepting a child's excuses for misbehavior, these stepparents fear their stepchild will never grow up to be a responsible adult.

Stepparents often believe that biological parents see their children through rose-colored glasses. Based on this belief, the stepparent may try to open the biological parent's eyes to the misbehavior of his or her children. In order to do so, the stepparent may "set the child up" or provoke him into being nasty in the presence of the biological parent. If the biological parent's rose-colored glasses aren't removed through the provocation of the stepchild at home, the stepparent may provoke the child to misbehave in a public setting, thinking the exhibition will surely convince the biological parent that his or her children are not perfect.

The unwillingness of a stepchild to accept a stepparent's authority plays a major role in the stepparent's harsh reaction to the stepchild. When the stepparent expresses commands, or even requests, gently, they often go unheeded, especially if the biological parent is lenient. When his or her request is ignored, the stepparent's most natural choice (although not the wisest) is to begin stating things more straightforwardly and with stronger emotion. And not only does the stepparent have to state the request; he also has to display the authority that allows him to state it.

"I asked you nicely to take out the trash; you ignored me. I am the head of this household. And as the head of this household I am now *telling* you to take out the trash."

Loudly stating your request, at the same time displaying your authority, is a bad habit to fall into. It seldom brings the long-term results you really want. Yes, at the moment you just want the child to obey. But the preferable long-term result is for your stepchild to obey out of respect for you as a person, as well as out of respect for your positional authority.

When co-parenting is at work in the household, the stepparent operates in authority with the biological parent and does not need to establish his or her own authority aggressively.

A low level of empathy on the part of the stepparent toward his or her stepchildren may also lead to harshness in discipline, with the stepparent failing to take sufficient time to gain understanding of the stepchild or hear the other side of the story. The stepparent's rigid adherence to the rules, with no exceptions allowed, is evidence he or she has accepted harshness or coldness as an "all right" disciplinary behavior.

Just as some biological parents' leniency may be directly attributed to their conflict style as peacekeepers, some stepparents who seem too harsh may be dominators by personality. They always want their way, be it with their stepchildren or their biological children, and they will nag, push and shove until they get it. If they don't, they will make life miserable for everyone. This is particularly evident in the arena of discipline and is obviously not co-parenting.

Some stepparents' harsh treatment of their stepchildren may reflect the pain and hurt they are experiencing because their mate's primary loyalty is to his or her biological children and not the couple relationship. Or the stepparent may be feeling like an outsider, and viewing everyone else in the family as "in." When the stepparent is hurt, his or her discipline often contains an element of revenge, a way of expressing his or her disillusionment by noticing, and pointing out, everything he or she thinks the stepchild does wrong.

Will the Family Member Who Is Really in Control Please Stand Up?

Blended families inevitably experience some confusion about who does what parenting. Both the biological parent and the stepparent may question whether they want to be viewed by the children as parents or as friends.

If the biological parent and/or the stepparent primarily assume the role of friend, the children control the home, creating absolute chaos.

If the biological parent primarily assumes the role of parent and the stepparent primarily assumes the role of friend, the biological parent is in control, which may leave the stepparent feeling like an outsider.

If the biological parent primarily assumes the role of friend and the stepparent primarily assumes the role of parent, all havoc breaks loose, radically increasing the tension and conflict in the home.

If together the biological parent and the stepparent primarily assume the role of parent, they present structure, a united front.

Children in Control

There are several reasons the children control some blended family households, leaving the family structure in a shambles.

1. During the single-parent household years, many single parents relate to their children as peers or friends. The children begin assuming that equal status means equal authority. Combined with our current societal belief system that everything is relative or subjective, the children then view themselves as "free agents" who do not have to subject themselves to parental authority.

2. Children learn at an early age how to confuse their parents. They are also intelligent enough to discover that once their parents are confused, they can be rendered powerless in discipline.

Children's tactics are very basic: They make statements such as "That's not fair" and "Everybody's doing it," in hopes Mom and/or Dad will wonder if in fact they are being unfair, old-fashioned, mean, ugly and senile.

Blended family children also have their basic ploys for attempting to control parents and stepparents. Their favorite statements are "You're only making me do this because he [the stepparent] told you to make me do it," "I'll move in with Mom" or "I don't have to do that at Dad's."

3. Biological parents often give in to their children's demands for fear of losing the parent/child relationship. Children may continually put their parents into situations where they have to prove the quality and strength of their love. Because the biological parent doesn't want his or her child to think, *You've chosen someone else over me,* children usually have their way in loyalty conflict situations.

4. Frequently the biological parent views the stepparent/ stepchild relationship as so fragile that any expression of disapproval shown toward the stepchild on the part of the stepparent is immediately thwarted by the biological parent. In this attempt to smooth things over, the biological parent often ends up explaining away the stepparent's role as a parent.

5. By nature some biological parents and stepparents are peacekeepers. When the peacekeeping parent allows children to continue in inappropriate behavior, that parent has become an enabler.

While this is all happening in one household, you can almost count on its happening in the child's other household. After a few years of both households accommodating little Johnny and Susie, we've turned them into dominating monsters who, if they don't get their way, will perform whatever behavior is necessary to win.

Children acquire control of the household when both the biological parent and the stepparent have primarily assumed the role of friend. They may assume that role due to triangulations, coalitions, lack of parental priorities and the biological parent's fear of loss and feelings of guilt.

When children have too much power in the blended family system, the stepparent remains an outsider, the blended family as a unit stops growing and the family goes from crisis to crisis.

In our society and in our blended families, we've worried so much about children's rights that we have neglected our responsibilities as parents. We have acted as if our children know as much about life as we do, or as if they possess the ability to make adult decisions. We forget they are children caught in gratifying their current emotional needs, and are, for the most part, unmindful of long-term consequences.

Children need to understand that they are equal as human beings who deserve to be treated with dignity and respect, but they are not equals when it comes to authority.

When the biological parent primarily assumes the role of parent and the stepparent primarily assumes the role of friend, the stepparent feels powerless and ineffective as a family member. When attempts made by the stepparent to fulfill the parental role are continually blocked by the biological parent, everyone in the family views the stepparent as the outsider who just happens to live in this house.

Biological parents may send their mates a mixed message: "Please support and nurture my children, but I'll handle discipline." If children know their stepparent is disciplinarily powerless, they will use that fact to their advantage to get what they want. The result? There will be no united front in either discipline or nurture. If the stepparent feels his or her mate doesn't trust him or her enough to discipline the children, what point is there in expending energy to be a nurturing parent?

When the biological parent primarily assumes the role of friend and the stepparent primarily assumes the role of parent, nobody's happy. The biological parent often sides with his or her friends (the children) against the bad guy (the stepparent). The stepparent, who thinks he or she is really contributing to the family, is dumfounded to discover that everyone, including his or her mate, is angry.

What Does It Take to Co-Parent?

In order for both the biological parent and the stepparent to assume the role of parent and to co-parent as a couple, they need to adopt a parental attitude, develop a discipline plan and present a united front.

Adopting a Parental Attitude

A parental attitude is easier when you understand the following job description. As a parent to all of the children in your blended family you are to:

- Express love and affection toward your children.

- Set an example.

- Be consistent.

- Develop your children's self-esteem.

- Give your children a sense of belonging in the family.

- Teach your children to be responsible.

- Train your children spiritually.

- Be responsible for your children's education.

- Treat your children with respect and require respect in return.

- Discipline your children.

Developing a Discipline Plan

Parents in blended families can seldom respond spontaneously to children's misbehavior. When they do, the leniency/harshness dichotomy often comes to the forefront, further perpetuating conflict in the home.

It is crucial, therefore, that blended families have a discipline plan they can adhere to consistently. This plan must include general household rules everyone in the family follows. If, when formulating this discipline plan, the biological parent and stepparent operate as team builders, it is more likely the entire family will benefit.

When setting up the household rules and consequences for breaking them, be sure you believe in what you are agreeing to. Only when you believe in the rules will you follow through with the consequences, thus proving your reliability to both your mate and your children.

Presenting a United Front

If parental interaction with children is to benefit the entire family, neither mate can defect from the discipline plan agreed upon. Defection on the part of either mate destroys the united front so important to successful family living.

Mates defect from agreed-upon disciplinary plans for several reasons. These may not be obvious to the one defecting, but they are glaringly conspicuous to the mate.

1. *A mate may unwittingly base child-rearing decisions on his or her "mood for the day."* If a good mood prevails, the children get off easy. If a bad mood prevails, the kids will be lucky to be grounded only a week.

Moods are inconsistent. When they wear off, a parent frequently realizes he or she made a poor disciplinary decision and changes his or her stance, often without consulting the mate.

"When I agreed the children should be in bed by eight-thirty, I was upset with them. I'm not in a bad mood anymore, so it really doesn't count."

Anytime disciplinary agreements or decisions are based more on emotions than reason, parents show an inconsistency in child-rearing that breeds distrust between mates and misbehavior in children.

2. *Sometimes a mate's personality type and conflict management style affect his or her reactions and commitment to a disciplinary plan.*

An escape artist may refuse to acknowledge an obvious problem.

A peacekeeper will agree to anything to maintain peace momentarily.

A dominator may say things even he or she recognizes as gross overstatements on an actual position.

A deal maker may work out a temporary deal, willing, at the time, to lose a little to gain a little. Later, however, he or she may say, "Why on earth did I ever agree to that?"

3. *Occasionally a mate may mean what he or she says, but reserve the unspoken right to break a promise if there are extenuating circumstances.*

Sam and Tessie, for example, agreed on a specific household rule pertaining to eating what is served at mealtime: Any family member who refused to eat what was served would not be allowed to eat again until the next meal. No snacks would be offered between meals and no special foods would be substituted for the meal already prepared.

Sam and Tessie agreed on this rule in principle. Then one day Tessie's son, Mikey, refused to eat the chicken dish Tessie had made for dinner. Tessie felt these were extenuating circumstances. Her thought process ran something like this:

"Mikey is such a picky eater, and he's so thin. If I can get him to eat anything I feel I've done my duty as a mother. Besides, I forgot how much he hates chicken. I knew he was going to eat dinner with the family tonight; why didn't I make something else? If I can just sneak him a freezer pizza or a fast-food burger later, I'll feel much better. The boy doesn't have an ounce of fat on his body to keep him going until breakfast."

4. *Then there are times when a mate intentionally defects from the discipline plan.* He or she understands the agreement fully,

but also knows he or she will not follow through with the consequences.

Vernon's situation is a good example.

"My wife has been nagging. She's been harping. She's threatened to throw all of my clothes out on the driveway unless I agree on some basic rules for my son's use of the car. She says it's never home when she needs it, or if it is, it's out of gas.

"Now that we've agreed on some rules, she's stopped nagging, harping and threatening. My son and I have a basic understanding—what his stepmother doesn't know won't hurt her. He can take the car anytime he wants while she's at work, as long as he replaces the gas he used. And if he needs a couple of dollars to do that, he can come see me."

The underlying, unconscious motivation for many of these behaviors stems from loyalty conflicts. Knowing what you believe, what your responsibilities are as a parent and co-parenting with your mate concerning discipline issues will help you avoid allowing misplaced loyalties to deter you from doing what is best for everyone in your blended family.

Remember: Every time you defect from the co-parenting agreement, you prove yourself unreliable and untrustworthy. When you are unpredictable, say things you really don't mean, reserve the right to break your promises or agreements or are dishonest, your mate will not trust you. If your mate cannot rely on your word, he or she, more often than not, will prefer to deal with discipline alone rather than to co-parent.

Trust between mates as well as between all family members produces less anger, suspicion and conflict. As one biological parent stated, "It doesn't bother me when my husband corrects my children, because I don't take it personally. I know he's disciplining them for something they did, and because he cares about them. I'm not wondering if he thinks I didn't train my children properly or if he sees me as an inadequate parent."

Some time ago, Adrienne roused me from a sound sleep, saying, "I just had the strangest dream."

"Can't it wait until morning?" I asked.

"It *is* morning. It's five A.M. Come on. Wake up."

Knowing my wife wouldn't give up, I sat up and tried to focus as she talked.

"In this dream I was a teacher again. It was mid-semester and my first day of teaching high school. As the students came trickling in for my first class, their previous teacher walked through the door with them, chatting and joking. She walked over to my desk and started shuffling through the papers and books there—*her* papers and books! In fact, everything in the room was hers, from the gradebook to the charts and posters on the wall.

"When the bell rang, she busied herself at the back of the room. I began to teach, but the students kept interrupting me, asking dumb questions and bringing the other teacher into the conversation. The class became more and more unruly as she interjected comments and the students began to ignore my presence totally.

"Tom, it was awful. I had no control over my students, my classroom or this disruptive teacher. I knew she was checking up on me. She couldn't stand the thought of leaving me alone in 'her' classroom with 'her' students. As their ex-teacher she was positive I wasn't capable of teaching them as she could. She didn't trust me.

"At the end of the class hour I didn't like any of my students, I despised their ex-teacher, I was very unhappy with my own performance as an educator and I had a horrendous tension headache."

As I listened to Adrienne I couldn't help but say, "So now you know how a stepparent feels."

When biological parents do not trust the stepparent with their children, they may respond as the teacher in Adrienne's dream did. They may side with their children, continually discredit the stepparent in disciplinary matters and make decisions for the children that may affect the stepparent without consulting the stepparent.

There is another side to the coin. In order to be trusted you have to be trustworthy. A young woman with whom I counseled some time ago had just separated from her husband when she came to see me. Within two weeks of their separation her ten-year-old son began telling her defiantly, "So what if you won't let me do what I want to do? I can do whatever I want at Dad's."

The very next time her estranged husband came to pick up their son, she sat down with him in their son's presence and described the boy's attitude and comments.

Her husband responded the way she trusted he would. He calmly but firmly informed their son that if he could not do something in his mother's house, he was not allowed to do it in his dad's house. Then he carried it one step further: "If you are grounded from the TV or telephone in your mother's house, you will experience the same consequences in my home."

Although this woman and her husband obviously had their difficulties, he had proven himself reliable in the past when it came to parenting their son.

Co-Parenting and the Other Household

Trust is an important element in co-parenting, whether with your mate or the other household. Like it or not, trust and co-parenting with the other household begin with *you* and *your reliability*. It is much easier to change the other household's concept of your reliability than it is to change the other household. When you work on being reliable, the other household will begin to view you as more reliable and trust you more, thus increasing the possibility of their willingness to co-parent with you.

Once you have established your reliability by picking the children up and bringing them home when you promised, considering the other household's plans or vacation dates when planning your family activities or vacations and paying your child support on time, you can begin expecting the other household to be reliable.

Each time the other household acts reliably, let them know clearly how much you appreciate it and why.

"I really appreciate your sending dress clothes with the children this weekend as we discussed over the telephone," or, "Thank you for calling me about Mark's report card. I appreciate your willingness to share your concern about his grades with me."

When the other household acts unreliably, say so just as clearly. But don't act as if they have committed the unforgivable sin. Treat each specific instance of unreliability as an opportunity for problem-solving through collaboration.

Suppose the other household is late picking the children up for visitation. Try saying, "The children and I have been waiting forty-five minutes for you to pick them up. It would be better for all of us if we knew exactly when you are going to come. That way they will be less anxious and I will be less upset. Perhaps we have just had a misunderstanding. Would it be better if I called you next Saturday morning before you come to make sure we both have the right time? Or could you call me if you are running late so I can reassure the children you are still coming? What do you think?"

By dealing with the other household's unreliability in this manner, you have practiced team-building techniques. Perhaps they will be late less often in the future, or at least will call if they are going to be.

Often we don't want to co-parent with the other household because its members have different values or we don't approve of their conduct. To show our disapproval we may cut off communication and try to keep the children with us as much as possible. We will have a much greater influence on the other household, however, by proving our reliability to them than by cutting off communication altogether.

According to a study by Lutz in 1983, *Family Relations* (pp. 367–375), the three top stressors experienced by teenagers in blended families are: biological parents talking negatively about each other; arguments between the biological parent and stepparent; not being allowed to visit the other biological parent.

Children need contact with both parents. Children are the reason for maintaining a good working relationship between households. When both households work together to parent their children, they establish stability in their children's lives, minimize loyalty conflicts and give their children the sense of security they desperately need.

In order to reach the goal of raising healthy children, mates need to work together as co-parents in their own household and as co-parents with the other household.

In wrapping up this chapter we would like to share some basic principles on parenting, co-parenting with your mate and co-parenting with the other household.

Basic Parenting Principles

Principle 1: Treat children with respect and require that they respect you.

Principle 2: Apply natural and logical consequences when appropriate.

Principle 3: Allow children to make age-appropriate choices and let them experience the consequences of those choices.

Principle 4: Have a discipline plan and follow it.

Principle 5: Communicate the plan to your children.

Principle 6: Be consistent.

Principle 7: Never administer discipline when you are emotionally upset.

Principle 8: Children do not have to agree with the whys of discipline. Just define the rules and administer the consequences.

Principle 9: Whether you are a biological parent or a stepparent, a custodial parent or a noncustodial parent, don't let emotions such as guilt or fear stop you from being a responsible parent.

Basic Principles of Co-Parenting with Your Mate

Principle 1: Develop a discipline plan with your mate using the techniques of a team builder.

Principle 2: Do not defect from the discipline plan.

Principle 3: If you don't want your mate to be too harsh with your children, don't be too lenient with them.

Principle 4: If you don't want your mate to be too lenient with his or her children, don't be too harsh with them.

Principle 5: When the biological parent is reprimanding or pointing something out to his or her children, the stepparent should not interject.

Principle 6: When the stepparent is reprimanding his or her stepchildren, the biological parent can interject, but should not undermine the stepparent's discipline.

Principle 7: Always remember that your mate's children are precious to him or her. When you speak ill of the cub or attack the cub, you can be sure the bear will come after you.

Basic Principles for Co-Parenting with the Other Household

Principle 1: Keep the other household informed concerning the children's activities, events, accomplishments and misbehaviors. Although you cannot expect the other household to enforce your consequences for misbehaviors that happened in your household, keeping them informed allows them that option.

Principle 2: Be supportive of the parenting in the other household. If your child returns to your home complaining about being grounded, don't degrade the other parent's discipline style in front of your child. If you have a problem with the way discipline is being handled in the other household, talk with the other household, not your children. They may not change their parenting style, but you have at least addressed an area where there is a clear difference in parenting.

Principle 3: Help your children identify with the positive qualities in the other household. If the other household emphasizes athletics while yours emphasizes academics, encourage your children in both areas. Don't make it an "either/or" situation.

Principle 4: Accept your children as members of two house-

holds, and remember their need to belong in both households
. . . not just yours.

We would like to recommend you read the following
books on child-rearing: *Systematic Training for Effective Parenting* by Don Dinkmeyer, Ph.D., and Gary D. McKay,
Ph.D.; *Making Children Mind without Losing Yours* by Kevin
Leman; and *Dare to Discipline, The Strong-Willed Child* and
Parenting Isn't for Cowards, all by Dr. James Dobson.

— 11 —
Survivors

Joel, a husband, biological father and stepfather, commented, "My wife and I get along so well as a couple when the children are out of the house for the day or weekend."

Have you, like Joel, observed this blended family phenomenon? The life cycle of a nuclear family begins with the development of the couple relationship. For the remarried couple with children, the early days of marriage are often filled with family business and conflict. This does not negate or lower the need to develop the couple bond: It only makes the task more difficult, demanding conscious effort.

Surviving as a Couple

You can do several concrete things to strengthen and enhance your couple relationship.

1. *Make your couple relationship a top priority*. Attend a marriage seminar or workshop once a year. Read books on marriage aloud to each other and discuss them. Schedule time on your calendars to do things together as a couple . . . without

the children. View those scheduled times as appointments that cannot be broken.

2. *Be supportive of your mate*. The stepparent needs to be told he is doing a good job. The biological parent needs to be reassured that, although the stepparent may not have the same intensity of feelings toward his stepchildren as the biological parent, he will be supportive. Let your mate know he or she is appreciated.

Reassure your mate you have no interest in the ex. He or she is the other parent of your children and your contacts should concern only your children's welfare. When talking with your children's other parent on the phone or in person, limit your conversation to children's issues.

3. *Be empathetic toward your mate*. Empathy is the capacity to participate in another person's ideas or feelings, to understand another person and to look at the world through his or her eyes. Empathy, then, is not being detached from your mate, but rather being "with" him or her.

Empathy says:

"I respect you."

"I value you."

"You are important enough to me that I want to understand you."

And, "What you feel is so important to me that I will take the time to listen closely to what you say."

Empathy has two components: a) gaining understanding and b) communicating that understanding.

You have to *want* to gain understanding of your mate. When you dialogue, try to comprehend exactly what he or she is saying. During the course of the conversation:

· Do not add to what your mate is saying; "Boy, if my daughter hurt me the way your daughter hurt you, I'd be so angry."

· Do not subtract from what your mate is saying; "Oh, come on, now. It's not all that bad!"

· Do not change what your mate is saying; "You don't really mean that. What you really mean is. . . ."

It's not enough to understand how your mate feels. You need to *communicate* that understanding to him or her. You must be able to identify clearly for your mate that you have listened and that you understand. The greater the empathy, the greater the understanding.

4. *"Do not let the sun go down while you are still angry, and do not give the devil a foothold"* (Ephesians 4:26–27). The enemy can get a foothold in your marital and blended family relationships when you fail to resolve conflicts "before the sun goes down."

Let's use an imaginary couple, Oliver and Fran, to better understand the pattern unresolved conflict usually follows.

While Oliver and Fran are out to dinner with friends, Oliver makes a derogatory comment about Fran's daughter, Jeanetta. Fran's feelings are hurt and she can feel herself pulling back emotionally in her relationship with Oliver. Because she doesn't want to create a scene in the restaurant, however, Fran decides not to say anything to Oliver at that moment. But the longer she sits there, the more hurt and upset she becomes.

When Oliver and Fran take leave of the other couple, Fran is still stewing over Oliver's comment. Right then she could say, "Oliver, I can't stand it when you make negative remarks about Jeanetta, especially in public. It hurts me deeply, and I wish you wouldn't do it."

Based on Oliver's response, Fran's honesty about her feelings could end the tension. If Oliver made a caring response, the whole problem could be resolved, allowing the enemy no chance to damage the relationship.

If Oliver made such uncaring remarks as "You are just too sensitive" or "If Jeanetta would shape up, I wouldn't have to say things like that," he would only be perpetuating the tension. Further discussion, however, could still resolve the issue.

Should Fran elect to say nothing, her internal turmoil would continue to grow. At this point she might begin questioning her role in her relationship with Oliver, asking herself, "What am I supposed to do now?" or, "Does a wife have to put up with this?" This would still be an excellent time for Fran to express how she feels.

What happens if Fran doesn't get her feelings out in the open? First, all of Oliver's irritating habits, which Fran used to be able to overlook, now bother her.

Suppose Oliver made his derogatory comment at about 5:30 P.M. and Fran thought about it all evening. Now it's midnight and Fran and Oliver have gone to bed. Usually Oliver's snoring, tossing and turning don't bother Fran. Nor does his taking more than his share of the covers. But tonight love no longer covers a multitude of sins. His snoring and "flipping and flopping" are extremely irritating. And his "stealing" the covers is making her absolutely livid.

By morning Fran, still talking to herself, is thinking angrily, *Why does he have to push that snooze button so many times? Why can't he just get out of bed when the alarm goes off like a normal person? He's taking too long in the shower. He always takes too long in the shower. There he goes, chewing with his mouth open again. And why can't he take his elbows off the table?*

In fact, everything Oliver does from now on is going to get on Fran's nerves. At this point she is no longer angry about the incident: She is angry at the whole person, Oliver.

No longer does she view Oliver's remark as the problem. Instead she views Oliver as the problem.

What could have been a calm exchange with great conflict resolution possibilities has evolved into a major crisis that will take hours or even days to get over. This type of tension-building conflict is not limited to the couple relationship. Children or stepchildren can and often do say things that hurt our feelings. If we allow those hurts to go unresolved for any length of time, we will follow the same pattern Fran did.

Sit down as soon as possible with your mate, your children or your stepchildren when you have been hurt or are feeling tension in that relationship, and begin to talk it out in order to resolve the conflict.

To keep the enemy from getting a foothold in your marital relationship and your blended family, identify your feelings based on what took place, don't attack the other person, allow the other person to save face (the other person does not have to be made to feel like a fool in order to correct the situation) and look for solutions.

Focusing on the couple relationship is not only beneficial for the couple, but for the children as well. By observing a healthy marital relationship, your children will learn how a husband and wife should treat each other, how to collaborate and how important openness and honesty are in marriage.

In Summary

In chapter 1, we discovered that even the people who have been referred to as "the Christian experts on blended families" experience conflict in their blended families (and on national TV, no less!).

In chapter 2, we began to better understand the complexity of the blended family suprasystem and the conflict that goes with it. Although we may not like all the facts, what a relief it is to learn we are not alone!

In chapters 3 and 4, we read about the biological and step-parents' resentments. Our goal? To understand not only our own resentments, but our mate's as well.

Through reading chapter 5 on children's resentments we tried to better understand what previously may have appeared to be immature behavior on the part of our children.

In chapter 6 we learned that before we can start building, or rebuilding, our families, we must let go of past failures and mistakes and create an atmosphere of forgiveness at home. This atmosphere should contain a willingness to forgive and be forgiven.

Chapter 7 identified the characteristics of a healthy family. We learned that it is difficult for warm, caring emotions to grow out of chaos and that structure is essential for a healthy family life.

In chapter 8 loyalty conflicts were described as the greatest unconscious cause of disruption in blended families. We were encouraged to make the couple relationship, not the cross-generational or previous (ex-mate) loyalties, primary.

Chapter 9 described the five conflict styles, with the goal of helping us determine which styles our family members and the other household use most frequently. We studied the characteristics of the team builder, and how to collaborate, and saw team building as the best style to resolve conflict.

In chapter 10, we were introduced to co-parenting. We looked at the leniency vs. harshness dichotomy, the necessity for a discipline plan and how defecting from it undermines the plan, the family and the marriage. We also looked briefly at co-parenting with the other household and basic parenting and co-parenting principles.

For this book to be most beneficial, you need to put into

practice what you have read. We would like to suggest you do just that by following a few recommendations.

1. *If you have decided the primary loyalty should be to the couple relationship, draw a triangle, cut it out and put it on your refrigerator.* Use it as a constant reminder to check whether or not each day's battles are due to a loyalty conflict. To help you decide, ask, "Do I feel caught between two people who are vying for my loyalty?" or, "Am I putting someone else in a loyalty conflict?" Then deal with the loyalty issue using the steps we suggested.

2. *Accept that the biological parent will love his or her children more than the stepparent will.* As the stepparent gives the biological parent permission to love his or her children freely, the stepparent will feel more freedom to show love and affection toward them as well. The biological parent can then stop feeling guilty because he or she feels more for his or her biological children than for his or her stepchildren.

This is not to say, however, that unfair treatment between stepsiblings is acceptable. If you visit Washington, D.C., and want to bring back T-shirts with a picture of the White House on them for your children, buy them for all of the children in your blended family, not just your biological children.

3. *Individually define your values.* Define your parenting values in relationship to bedtimes, chores, keeping bedrooms clean, language, school performance, extracurricular activities, dating, using the family car and other similar issues.

Clearly define the values you would like for your family life, using the list of eleven characteristics of a healthy family as a guideline (see pp. 119–121).

4. *Compare your values with your mate's.* Where they differ, use team-building techniques to come up with a value statement for each issue that satisfies both of you.

5. *Type or write out a shortened version of the ten attitudes of a*

team builder and put them on the refrigerator next to your triangle.
List Frydenger & Frydenger's Seven Steps to Conflict Resolution (see page 152) and make three copies, one for home, one for his wallet and one for her purse. Then whenever and wherever you are, you can work out a conflict from that perspective.

6. *Decide on a discipline plan as a couple through team building; then stick with it.* Decide to be reliable. Mean what you say, and put action behind your words.

7. *Call a family meeting, which is described in detail in chapter 9 of* The Blended Family. Using that format, briefly explain to the children what you have learned about the inherent chaos in the blended family system and the resentments that can come out of it. Apologize for all of the things that have gone wrong and identify for the children that you want to work together, as a family, to improve your family life.

Again using the family meeting format from *The Blended Family,* ask your children to brainstorm about what they think makes a family happy and healthy. Have the eleven characteristics of a healthy family with you during the meeting as a reference. Let the children exhaust their ideas before you bring up these characteristics. Then develop a plan to implement the solution.

Implementing the steps described in this book will not be easy. Your family life will not change overnight. But with love for each other and determination, and faith in God and His power to help, your blended family can achieve a healthy and happy family life.

Bibliography

Fisher, Roger and Scott Brown. *Getting Together, Building Relationships As We Negotiate.* New York: Penguin Books, 1989.

Heitler, Susan M., Ph.D. *From Conflict to Resolution.* New York: W. W. Norton & Company, 1990.

Lutz, P. "The Stepfamily: An Adolescent Perspective." *Family Relations.* Vol. 32 No. 3. The National Council on Family Relations, July 1983, pp. 367–375.

Perlmutter, Barry F., John Touliatos, and A. Murray. *Handbook of Family Measurement Techniques.* Sage Publications, 1990.

Sager, C. J., et al. *Treating the Remarried Family.* New York: Brunner/Mazel, 1983.

Visher, Emily B. and John S. Visher. *Old Loyalties, New Ties, Therapeutic Strategies with Stepfamilies.* New York: Brunner/Mazel, 1988.